BOOK OF
CHOCOLATES & OTHER
EDIBLE GIFTS

Harrods
BOOK OF
CHOCOLATES & OTHER EDIBLE GIFTS

BY
Gill Edden

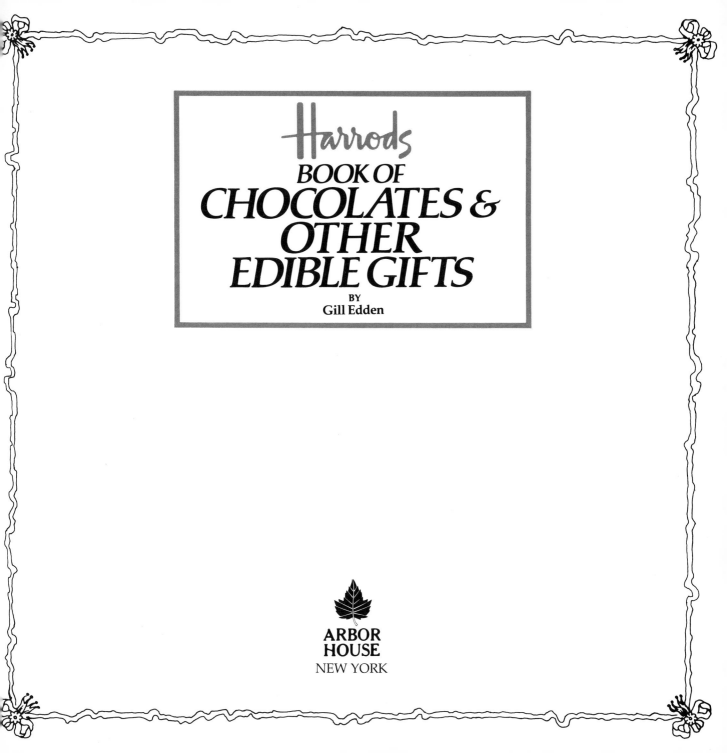

ARBOR
HOUSE

NEW YORK

First Impression 1986

Published in the United States of America by
Arbor House Publishing Company
and in Canada by Fitzhenry & Whiteside Ltd
by arrangement with Ebury Press, London

EDITORS: Fiona MacIntyre, Barbara Croxford, Susan Friedland
ART DIRECTOR: Frank Phillips
DESIGNER: Marshall Art
PHOTOGRAPHY: Grant Symon
STYLIST: Sue Russell
HOME ECONOMISTS: Susanna Tee, Janet Smith and Maxine Clark

Ebury Press would like to thank Harrods, and their archivist
Margaret Baber, for allowing the use of the black and white
illustrations taken from Harrods catalogues.

Library of Congress Cataloging-in-Publication Data

Edden, Gill.
    Harrods book of chocolates and other edible gifts.

    1. Candy.   2. Chocolate candy.   I. Harrods Ltd.   II. Title.
TX791.E33   1986   641.8′53   86-8021
ISBN 0-87795-818-1

Contents

*All eggs used in this book are
large unless otherwise stated.*

Introduction

THE CONFECTIONER'S art is a frivolous pastime, deemed unnecessary in the serious world. Who, after all, needs to eat candy? But the fun of making them and the luxury of the results are their own reward.

Home-made chocolates, candies and petits fours will figure as a treat in any household, as much pleasure for the cook to create as for everyone to eat. And as an inexpensive, thoughtful gift, they must come top of the list.

It is an age-old custom to offer small gifts of food on special occasions. For birthdays, anniversaries and religious festivals such gifts are traditional. In some cases, even the form of the food required is traditional, such as the chocolate Easter egg or spiced Christmas cookies. There are other times, too, when a small gift is deemed appropriate, particularly when you are accepting hospitality. On such occasions as these, home-made chocolates, candies or petits fours draw a pleasing balance between a gift that is merely a token gesture and one that comes with genuine care and affection.

Most people's first experience of candy-making comes in childhood, as an entertainment on a wet afternoon. At that stage, the choice will usually be of uncooked candies that can be made simply, and without danger, by young inexperienced hands. These are a good introduction to the art, and will whet the appetite for more adventurous forays.

After uncooked candies, the next most common step is to fudges. The techniques of fudge-making are relatively forgiving; there are a variety of possible results, all of which are acceptable. If one member of the family likes a creamy fudge, another will like it crisp and candyish, so nothing can actually be considered "wrong." Shaping is easy and the sweet keeps quite well. As a gift, you can even pack fudge and send it by mail successfully. Fudge, therefore, provides a good confidence builder for the beginner in boiled sugar candy-making.

But as soon as you venture into the realms of boiled sugar, the task becomes more demanding. It requires patience, precision and a certain degree of dexterity. But still the fun remains – and even first attempts, which may not be as confidently executed and perfectly shaped as you might like, will give pleasure in the making and consumption.

For the family cook, toffees and hard candies, yield enormous fun. Traditional molasses toffee, old-fashioned humbugs, barley sugar sticks and fruit drops all appeal to children. The varied colors and shapes have an element of fantasy that are as important as their flavors. However, they are quite difficult to make. The high sugar temperatures required are dangerous with youngsters around, the syrup burns easily and handling techniques require practice before they can be totally successful. But the processes are fascinating, and pulled and twisted candies add another dimension to the confectioner's art.

Probably the most useful technique to master is that of fondant making. With a single batch of fondant, you can create both glistening fondant shapes and creamy centers for chocolates. You can even use fondant for icing cakes. It keeps well, too. You can make a large batch of the basic mixture to keep for several weeks and use for different purposes. Experiment to your heart's content with new flavors and delicate colors.

But of all types of confectionery, chocolates shine through, with the most impressive looking results for the least effort. The basic product comes to you ready made, and dipping, coating or molding are not difficult. Only the centers require imagination. The results, even for a beginner, are pure luxury.

Many preserves make popular edible gifts, but none are more luxurious than candied or glacé fruits. Candying is an attractive way of using seasonal fruits when there is a glut. They keep well, so there is no need to worry about finding a suitable recipient immediately. Candied fruits make an unusual standby gift to keep in your pantry – as long as you do not let the rest of the family know they are there, because if you do they will certainly disappear! Each type of fruit is best candied separately so take your time and prepare each kind in turn, ready to make up mixed boxes when gift time comes.

Petits fours are a more spur of the moment "make today, give tonight" gift. They make a perfect present to take with you to a dinner party, though it may be as well to tell your host or hostess first. Petits fours will always complete a party meal perfectly. The guests may think they have eaten well already, but a tempting sweet morsel served with the after dinner coffee is rarely refused. An attractive box of truffles or a gift wrapped plate of mixed plain and fancy petits fours is a pretty compliment to any cook.

INGREDIENTS

Sugar

Sugar is the single most important ingredient in confectionery – without it, few candies would exist. Granulated sugar is used for most recipes where the mixture is heated, but different types of brown sugar can be used in toffee and fudge recipes to vary the flavor. Superfine sugar can be used instead of regular granulated if you wish; it dissolves a little more quickly but otherwise will give no different results. Sugar cubes likewise will make no difference to the finished candy, but will cost you a little more. In uncooked recipes, you need to use fine confectioner's sugar to produce a smooth texture.

Other sweeteners, such as honey or corn syrup and acids such as vinegar, cream of tartar or lemon juice, are all used to control the re-crystallization of the melted sugar as it cools; the ingredients used depend on the recipe. Honey and corn syrup affect flavor as well, whereas the other additions affect only the size of the new crystals that form in the sugar as it cools. The quantity of these crystal "inhibitors" used in any recipe is crucial – alterations from the basic proportion will give a candy of a very different texture.

Flavorings

Modern cooks have an advantage over old-fashioned candy-makers in the wide range of bottled extracts and flavoring oils available. Without them, the distillation of concentrated flavorings, such as fruit juice, would be a long and time-consuming process. Just a few drops, or perhaps ½ teaspoon, of these extracts is enough to shine through the sweetness of the sugar without altering the texture of the basic mixture.

But do buy good-quality products. Generally, a label that proclaims "extract of" or "oil of" means the real product, whereas "flavoring" is likely to be a synthetic substitute. The difference is quite marked in use.

Colorings

Use food colorings sparingly or you will have garish results. If a recipe says "a few drops," it means maybe three or four drops, not a splash. Some bottles are fitted with dropper tops; otherwise dip a skewer into the bottle and shake the drops off the end of the skewer to control the amount you use. Never tip the bottle up over the candy mixture, in case you slip!

Fruit and nuts

It always pays to buy top-quality dried fruits. The flavors are much better than cheaper brands and the difference is noticeable in the finished candies. Nuts are best bought in the shell as these have maximum moisture and flavor. Next best are shelled but with the skins left on. Nuts which have been skinned, or worse still chopped or ground, before packing have too much surface exposed to the air; they will have dried out and lost a considerable amount of their flavor. Buy nuts in small quantities as and when you need them. The longer they sit in your cupboard, the more flavor they lose. Freeze nuts you don't plan to use immediately. Processors, packers and distributors are more likely to have suitable storage conditions than you are.

You will find that many of the recipes in this book suggest toasting nuts. This intensifies

the flavor so that it stands up better against the all-intrusive sweetness of such mixtures as fondant or fudge.

Chocolate

Almost any variety of chocolate can be used for home-made confectionery, depending on the recipe. Unsweetened chocolate, also called bitter or baking chocolate, contains only chocolate – the pure form of the cocoa liquor; semi-sweet chocolate, sometimes called bittersweet, contains sugar as well as extra cocoa butter; sweet chocolate, such as German chocolate (which can also be labeled sweet cooking chocolate), contains even more sugar than semi-sweet chocolate. All these chocolates are sold in packages containing 1-oz squares. Milk chocolate and chocolate chips (usually semi-sweet) are also used in confectionery. For dipped chocolates, it is best to use special, waxy candy-making chocolate.

If a recipe calls for semi-sweet chocolate, do not substitute sweet or unsweetened chocolate unless you know the exact sugar and cocoa butter content of the different chocolates, and can make allowances for these differences in the recipe.

Nonmilk chocolate tends to be easier to use than milk, possibly because of the presence of extra cocoa butter in the paler version. But white chocolate (which is not really chocolate but a vegetable oil mixture flavored with vanilla) can be used quite successfully. A selection of mixed milk, nonmilk and white chocolates looks attractive, but in practice most people seem to prefer to eat the milk or nonmilk versions.

◆ EQUIPMENT ◆

Very little special equipment is needed for making chocolates and other candies. A good, heavy saucepan and a wooden spoon are the most important items. A thermometer is the only piece of equipment I would recommend you buy especially for your first attempt at confectionery making. And you can even do without this, if you use the tried and tested cold water tests listed on page 15; however, they are less reliable than a thermometer until you have long experience of sugar boiling.

Saucepans

Use a heavy saucepan, always choosing one larger than the initial quantity of ingredients would seem to warrant. Most of the recipes in this book involving boiling sugar were made in 3- or 4-quart saucepans. Aluminum is the best material to use as it gives the most even heat distribution. Stainless steel is satisfactory as long as the base of the pan has a heavy aluminum or copper core, but there is a tendency for syrup at the sides of the pan to scorch so constant attention is required.

Enameled saucepans are not suitable, as the heat of boiling sugar may damage the surface.

Non-stick coatings on pans are equally fragile. In theory, an uncoated cast iron pan should be ideal, but in practice I find that the cast iron gets too hot too quickly, and the pan retains its heat too long after you remove it from the stove, making it almost impossible not to scorch the syrup. Use tin-lined copper pans if you are lucky enough to own them.

To clean a toffee-coated saucepan, do not struggle with harsh cleaners and steel wool. Simply fill the saucepan with fresh water and simmer until all the sugar has dissolved.

Thermometer

For sugar-boiling, the temperatures required range between about 200° and 350°, but the most useful thermometer is a multi-purpose candy thermometer graduated from 50° right up to 500° or more. You can use this for many cooking processes – from yogurt-making, through fruit canning and jam-making and on to deep fat frying. It should have a moveable clip to fasten it to the side of the saucepan. Choose a thermometer that has the bottom of the bulb protected, so that it does not come into direct contact with the base of the pan.

Do not put the thermometer in the syrup until all the sugar has dissolved, or you will risk grains of sugar clinging to the thermometer. Never plunge it straight into boiling syrup either or it may break – leave the thermometer standing in a mug of hot water to warm up until required. Equally do not take it out of boiling syrup and put it directly onto a cold surface or into cool water; a mug of boiling water will both protect the thermometer from the possible damage caused by a sudden temperature change and soak off the sticky sugar.

To take an accurate reading on a thermometer, always bend down and read it at eye level, taking care to be far enough away to protect your face from any splattering syrup. One or two degrees above or below the specified temperature will affect the finished candy, and the distortion caused by reading the thermometer from above is enough to spoil a batch of fondant or fudge.

Spoons and spatulas

Use a wooden spoon for stirring, so that the handle does not get hot, but have a metal spoon handy to check that the sugar has dissolved before you start to boil. Any residual grains of sugar in a syrup will be clearly visible on the surface of a metal spoon, though totally invisible on wood. Use a strong wooden spatula for working fondant.

Heat diffuser

Unless you are particularly lucky with the simmer controls on your stove, you will find a heat diffuser invaluable for achieving the low, even heat required for melting chocolate and fondant. These usually take the form of a double mat of pierced metal, with a handle for easy lifting.

left WALNUT CUPS (page 36); bottom CHOCOLATE HAZELNUT CLUSTERS (page 24); right SOFT ALMOND CENTERS (page 27)

Baking sheets

Marble is the traditional surface for cooling and working fondant and toffee. But few people have a large marble slab in the kitchen these days, and for large quantities you need retaining sides anyway. I use large enameled baking sheets, but they must be scrupulously clean. If the sheets have any traces of ancient baking on them, soak thoroughly first in a baking soda solution.

Pans

For most fudges and toffees, you need shallow square or oblong baking pans; foil dishes can be substituted for these. Oil them well before use to make turning out easier. The size most commonly used in this book is a 7-inch-square pan.

Molds

Molds for fondants and chocolates come in rubber or plastic sheets, flexible for easy turning out. Easter egg molds are also made of flexible plastic. They are readily available from cookware shops, department stores and suppliers of plastic freezer and microwave ware. But the easiest molds for chocolate are foil or paper cases that can be peeled off when the fragile shell is set, making pretty chocolate cups.

Cutters

You do not need a great range of fancy cutters, but one or two shapes of the right size will be useful. Cutters about ¾–1 inch in diameter are the most suitable. Look out for them in specialty cookware shops. If you do not have cutters the correct size, use a sharp knife and make square, diamond and oblong shapes which are just as effective.

Dipping ring and fork

A dipping ring is a small wire hoop with a wooden handle, used to hold the centers while you dip them in chocolate or fondant. A dipping fork is similar but open ended – I find the ring easier to use. Dipping rings and forks are easy enough to obtain in cookware shops but for occasional use or if you cannot obtain them substitute the wrong end of a skewer.

Rubber gloves

Professionals use their bare hands but, for a beginner, rubber gloves are the ideal protection when handling hot fondant or toffee.

Trivet

Saucepans containing boiling sugar become exceptionally hot. Protect your work surfaces with a trivet.

Paper

Baking parchment, with a slightly waxed finish, is the best surface for drying most candies and for packing between layers of sweets in a box. Wax paper can be used if that is all you have on hand.

TECHNIQUES

Sugar boiling

The techniques of sugar boiling are fundamental to the art of the confectioner. If the basic syrup is wrong, no amount of shaping and decorating can disguise it.

Start by choosing a mild, dry day for candy-making. Heat or cold, or a damp or humid atmosphere will all spoil the results. Toffees will be sticky and fondants will refuse to set.

Using a heavy saucepan, of a size that allows plenty of room for the boiling sugar to rise in the pan, dissolve the sugar slowly over a gentle heat. Stir the mixture all the time as the sugar dissolves and do not allow it to come to a boil while there are still crystals present. If necessary at this stage, you can move the saucepan on and off the heat to prevent it from boiling, but it is preferable to use a heat diffuser. Stir with a wooden spoon so that you can leave the spoon in the pan without the handle becoming hot, but when you think the sugar is dissolved, check with a metal spoon. Scrape the bottom of the pan and go well into the corners to check that there are no crystals remaining. If there are any crystals left, they will show clearly on the metal spoon.

Once the sugar is dissolved, put in the thermometer, clipping it to the side of the pan, and turn up the heat. The sugar should boil fairly fast to the required temperature but avoid turning the heat too high at first or the syrup may burn. A steady, moderate heat is better than a fluctuating one. Do not stir once the sugar has boiled unless the recipe specifically says that you should – stirring will cause the sugar to re-crystallize, which in most cases will spoil the finished candies.

Recipes that include milk, cream or butter may need stirring occasionally as the milk solids are liable to burn on the bottom of the pan unless disturbed from time to time. Draw the wooden spoon carefully across the bottom of the pan and if there are no signs of sticking, leave it alone.

From time to time while the sugar is dissolving and boiling, brush around the sides of the saucepan with a pastry brush dipped in water. This will dissolve any grains of sugar that form on the sides of the pan above the general level of the syrup – these too could spoil the whole batch if allowed to remain. Professional confectioners achieve the same result by putting a lid on the pan, so that steam condenses and runs down the sides of the saucepan. (I prefer to be able to see what I am doing.)

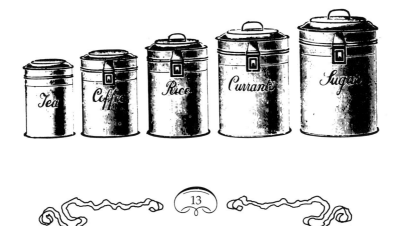

The sugar-boiling process requires extreme patience. It often takes a good hour for the quantities used in this book to reach the required temperature. And you cannot go away and leave the pan, as you would with a simmering stew or stock, because boiling sugar rises so readily in the pan and may quickly boil over. The temperature is extremely high and the hot spilled syrup is dangerous – as dangerous as boiling oil. Watch the thermometer closely as the correct temperature approaches and if it is rising very quickly, lower the heat to control the rise, or it may boil over the top even as you watch.

As soon as the thermometer registers the correct temperature, remove the pan from the heat. Do not just turn off the heat source – the cook top itself will still be hot and may continue to push up the temperature. Take the saucepan off the stove and place it on a trivet until the bubbles have subsided. Some people like to dip the base of the pan in cold water to cool it more quickly. As soon as the bubbles subside, pour the syrup into the pan, or follow the recipe instructions.

How you handle the sugar when it comes off the heat has as much effect on the finished candy as how you handle it during boiling. A mixture that is stirred or beaten while still very hot will quickly grain, or re-crystallize, and if you are not careful may well set before you can turn it out of the pan. This is how you achieve a crisp non-creamy fudge, for example.

So, for a clear, shining toffee or hard candy, do not stir at all after boiling. Simply pour the hot syrup into the prepared pan. For a candy that is to be opaque but still smooth textured, stir lightly. Leaving the mixture to cool somewhat before stirring lessens the effect and gives you more control; try this if you like a smooth, creamy fudge, not too grainy. For many fudges, the stirring that is necessary during boiling, to stop the milk solids from burning, is sufficient in itself and once the mixture has cooled slightly you can pour it straight into the pan.

"Pulling" is another method of changing the appearance of boiled sugar. Many toffees and hard candy mixtures are first poured onto a cold pan, while still hot, and left until cool enough to handle. Then, when set firmly enough to be picked up in a sheet, you start to work the mixture with your hands. Fold the sheet of sugar sides to middle and pull it out, fold again and pull again. The more you fold, twist and pull, so the toffee turns from clear to opaque and silky looking and it gradually sets.

Fondant also depends on the method of working it after boiling to the correct temperature. For fondant, the mixture is tipped onto a cold surface and worked with a spatula until it becomes hard and crystalline. You then use the warmth of your hands to knead it to a smooth, fine texture.

The addition of honey, corn syrup, cream of tartar, vinegar or lemon juice to the basic syrup all contribute to regulating the size of the crystals in the finished candies.

Cold water tests

Never, ever, touch boiling sugar without first dropping it into cold water. None of the tests is totally accurate, but with experience you will be able to judge the temperature of the sugar from its appearance. Even if you have a thermometer, it is worth doing the tests from time to time, in case you drop and break the thermometer in the mid-

dle of a batch of candy! Take the saucepan off the heat while testing. The names given to the various stages very slightly from cook to cook.

Thread 215–220°. Dip two small spoons in cold water then quickly in and out of the syrup. The backs of the spoons will slide easily over each other, but a thread of syrup will form between them. This is a thin syrup suitable for fruit salads or for thinning fondant.

Soft ball 235–245°. Spoon a little syrup into a bowl of cold water. Leave it for a moment to cool then remove and roll the syrup between your fingers into a ball. At 235° the ball will be very soft and will flatten when you first take it out of the water. The higher the temperature, the firmer the ball becomes. This is the range of temperatures for fudge and fondant.

Hard ball 245–265°. Spoon a little syrup into cold water, then roll into a ball. The ball should be quite firm but not rock hard. Caramels, nougat and marshmallows are boiled to these temperatures.

Soft crack 270–290°. Spoon a little syrup into cold water. It should separate into small, hard pieces but should not be brittle. Use this range for toffees and some hard candies.

Hard crack 300–310°. Spoon a little syrup into cold water. It will separate into hard, brittle threads. At 310° the syrup will be starting to turn a light golden color. This high temperature is used for really hard toffees.

Caramel 320–325°. The syrup will be a rich golden color. At this stage it is used for praline and for brittle caramel decorations.

Beyond this temperature, the syrup gradually turns a very dark brown and then black, the sweetness goes and it will taste burned. This type of syrup is not used for confectionery, but is a coloring for gravies and dark fruit cakes.

STORAGE

Most home-made candies are best eaten fairly quickly after making; uncooked candy should be eaten within a few days. Certainly, sugar is a superb preservative, and there is little danger to health in eating cooked candies that have been made some time ago. But the appearance and general condition, even of cooked candies, does deteriorate quite quickly. Commercial confectionery has preservatives and stabilizers added, which help keep it in good condition for longer.

As far as possible, store candies in airtight containers. If you are giving them away as presents in non-airtight packages, leave the decorative packing until the last reasonable moment. Store different types of confectionery separately, to prevent cross-flavoring.

In particular, candies are affected by temperature and humidity. Toffee left in a cold place will go sticky very quickly, and one piece will irretrievably glue itself to the rest. Chocolate goes gray and dry looking in the cold, loosing that lovely glossy bloom that makes it so attractive. Heat will of course melt chocolate, and start sugar running. A cool room temperature of about 55–65° seems to be about the median.

Most candies are best separated from each other, either by individual bonbon cases, by wrapping paper or by layers of baking parchment or wax paper. Wrap toffees, caramels and hard candies individually in plastic wrap, or foil. Pack chocolates and softer candies flat in boxes, not more than two layers deep, with cardboard or parchment between the layers. This prevents

them from sticking to each other and the shapes from distorting. Fudge is one of the best-tempered candies in storage. It will emerge in good condition several weeks later, not quite as perfect as when it first went in, but certainly in better condition than any toffee or chocolate stored for the same length of time. Fondant keeps relatively well too, though losing the pristine, glittery finish it has when freshly made.

The only candies that are best not eaten immediately are caramels. These are best left for two to three days, perhaps up to a week, to mature. By then, a very soft caramel will have hardened up a little, harder ones will have become pleasantly chewy. Candied and glacé fruits keep for several weeks without noticeable deterioration too, if packed in flat layers between sheets of parchment.

➤ PACKING EDIBLE GIFTS ➤

All foods should be wrapped or properly stored as soon as they are made, to keep them in good condition. But leave gift wrappings until the last minute, so that they are absolutely fresh for the occasion. Certainly it is worth taking a little trouble with packaging because it can make all the difference to the finished result. If you think your candies look a little amateurish just wait until you have packed them up! Choose a pretty gift box, line it carefully and put the candies in individual bonbon cases before you pack them and, hey presto, they will become the most sophisticated of gifts.

Individual wraps
Good packaging materials specially designed for

confectionery are hard to find. Without doubt, dark brown wax paper cases and sheets of dark brown wax paper are the most enhancing, so do search in speciality shops. The sheets of brown wax paper are particularly elusive, so if you do track some down, buy a good stock. Plain bright colors also look good, especially if you use a different color for each type of candy in a selection. The least attractive are those most readily available – white wax cases with a floral design – but even these have their uses. Also available are colored foil cases, particularly pretty for chocolates. One or two in a selection add a sparkle to your gift.

It is advisable to buy ready made bonbon cases before you make the candies, to check on sizes. Some are rather small and you may need to choose a different cutter, or otherwise adjust the size of your candies to fit.

For hard candies, plastic wrap and foil are the best utility wrappings, but these do not look good in a gift box. Hard shiny candies such as toffee or clear mints look marvelous wrapped in cellophane, either plain or colored. The stiff, clear film enhances the shine of the candy and stays looking crisp and fresh. Baking parchment or wax paper can be wrapped into neat parcels around square or oblong candies, or you can use the traditional taffy wrap, twisting the paper in opposite directions at each end. Be sure to cut each square of paper or cellophane large enough; you need about twice the length of the candy.

Ordinary baking parchment or wax paper is rather plain and you may like to overwrap it with a strip of colored foil. This foil can be bought either as specially cut candy wrappers or in a large sheet, as gift wrapping paper. The former are

inclined to be small and you will find it less restricting to cut your own. Foil wraps can be used underneath cellophane too, for extra color with the shine.

Petits fours are more difficult to pack than candy, being on the whole larger and of more variable shape. Small, round petits fours cases are easy enough to find, but long ones (for instance, for éclairs) or slightly larger ones, are more difficult. Overcome this by making your own separators. Take a large sheet of baking parchment or wax paper and pleat it at intervals to provide a flat base for a row of cakes or pastries, with a wall of paper between each row.

Boxes and other containers

Stationers and department stores sell pretty gift boxes in all sorts of shapes, sizes and colors. These provide the simplest way of packing your gift of candy, tied with ribbon or gilt thread. If possible, choose shallow boxes that will take a single layer, or at most two layers, of candies. (Piling up consecutive layers will leave the bottom layer squashed out of shape.) Line the box with dark wax paper, if possible, or with a plain bright wrapping paper to tone with the outside of the box, or with a doily – white, gold or silver.

For less delicate candies, bright miniature shopping bags are a simple idea. Or you can make your own bag from a sheet of gift wrapping paper, choosing a simple envelope shape, hobo's bundle, cone, firecracker or any other shape or idea your imagination and talents will run to.

A simpler wrap can be made with ordinary kitchen disposables. Shallow foil freezer dishes, paper plates or ovenproof cardboard dishes can all be made to look pretty with a decorative lining and individual bonbon cases. Plastic wrap makes an effective utility cover, but cellophane looks better, wrapped smoothly over the top and fastened underneath with tape. Tie a ribbon around or fasten a self adhesive bow on top to finish off the gift.

Reusable containers make popular gift wrappings. A glass storage jar or painted tin may well cost you no more than a one-use gift box. It has the advantage of being airtight, to keep the candy in good condition for longer, and the recipient will be able to use the container afterwards. A ribbon bow and a gift card are all the trimmings needed.

A more elaborate choice, particularly suited to a gift of petits fours, fondants or chocolates, would be a pretty china plate or glass dish. Less obvious containers might include an individual cup and saucer or mug, a cut glass tumbler or small basket. In each case, the container itself makes the wrapper, with only a transparent film of cellophane and a ribbon needed for the finishing touch.

Chocolates

A BOX of home-made chocolates is probably the most glamorous of the edible gifts you might give, and yet in many ways chocolates are the easiest candy to make. You can be endlessly inventive with the centers, or you can use ready-made candied fruit or whole nuts. Whatever you use for centers, the dark glossy coating of chocolate will look inviting and sophisticated.

The easiest chocolate to use for home confectionery work is the type actually sold as "candy-making or coating chocolate." It will melt easily to a perfect working consistency. With this type of chocolate, dipping is easy, cups and molded shapes are strong and crisp. The flavor is just as good as that of dessert chocolate.

There is also a wide range of milk and nonmilk chocolates available. These are all more or less suitable, though nonmilk chocolate is generally easier to work with than milk. Baking chocolate melts to a dipping consistency less easily than candy-making chocolate, and it helps to add just a little pure vegetable margarine to thin it. A really tiny amount is enough – less than ½ tablespoon vegetable margarine will bring 8 oz baking chocolate to just the right consistency. Check the package carefully to make sure that you use *pure* vegetable margarine for this purpose – animal fats do not have the same effect.

You will find that most of the recipes in this chapter use semi-sweet or candy-making chocolate – semi-sweet giving the best flavor, candy-making the easiest coating.

To melt chocolate, break or grate it into a bowl and place over a saucepan of hot water. The bowl should not touch the water, and the water should not be allowed to boil – that way there is less danger of overheating the chocolate. Heat slowly and gently, stirring from time to time until it reaches a good coating consistency. Remove the saucepan from the heat and leave the bowl over the hot water to maintain the temperature. If you have a lot of work to do and the chocolate starts to cool and thicken again, just reheat carefully. The most important point is not to overheat the chocolate or the texture of the coating will be

CHOCOLATE WALNUT CREAMS (page 26)

spoiled. About 85° is the right temperature; a thermometer is not really necessary – judging by eye is quite satisfactory.

To ensure you achieve a good coating, do not be stingy with the chocolate. Use more than you think you will need rather than trying to skimp, and pick up a generous coating with each center you dip. Any left over at the end can be saved for cake decorating or for dessert or sauce-making.

For dipping, use a dipping ring or fork to hold the centers. For most shapes, the ring is more satisfactory, giving a firmer nesting place for the center. If the proper equipment seems to be unavailable in your area, the ring end of a skewer works quite well. After dipping, hold the chocolate over the bowl for a moment to let the excess run off, then wipe underneath the ring with a skewer. Place each chocolate carefully on a sheet of baking parchment or wax paper to dry, giving

each one a gentle push to cover the bottom completely. The slightly waxed surface of parchment makes it easier to lift the finished chocolate when it has hardened.

Finally, dry and store your chocolates at a cool room temperature of 55–65°. In too cold an atmosphere the chocolate quickly clouds over, losing its bloom and taking on a grayish look; too warm and it will melt again. It helps preserve the good looks if you put the finished chocolates in a box and cover them as soon as they are dry.

When packing chocolates for a gift, look for the dark brown wax paper bonbon cases, or brightly colored foil ones. These set off the chocolates to best advantage. The really large chocolates won't fit into cases anyway, but they look good displayed in a box lined with a doily. For the most attractive gift, make up a box of mixed centers rather than packing all one kind together.

Chocolate Orange Creams

The home-made candied peel on page 28 is ideal for decorating this traditional soft center chocolate. If you use purchased peel do be careful as the chopped mixed peel usually sold for cake making is very harsh flavored and quite unsuitable. At a top quality grocers, you can usually find candied peel in large pieces, which tastes quite good. Otherwise leave the chocolates plain or decorate with silver balls.

½ lb (1 cup) basic fondant
(see page 42)
3 drops orange extract
orange food coloring
7 oz milk chocolate

about ½ tablespoon
vegetable margarine
candied orange peel, to
decorate

MAKES ABOUT 12 OZ

Knead the fondant until pliable, gradually working in the orange extract and a very little coloring, just to tint it a pale orange. Roll out the fondant to about ½ inch thick on a board lightly dusted with confectioners' sugar. Cut out shapes, using the same cutter each time. Leave the fondants to dry on parchment paper.

When the centers are thoroughly dry, break the chocolate into a bowl and melt it over a pan of hot water. Add a little margarine if necessary to achieve a dipping consistency.

Using a dipping ring, dip the orange creams one at a time in the chocolate to give them a generous coating. Place on parchment. Before the chocolate dries, place a small piece of candied orange peel in the center of each one. Leave to dry.

Chocolate Ginger Creams

Fondant makes an excellent center for chocolate. It keeps well, is firm to dip, and is smooth and creamy when you bite.

½ lb (1 cup) basic fondant
(see page 42)
1½ teaspoons syrup from
a jar of preserved
ginger
7 oz semi-sweet chocolate

about ½ tablespoon
vegetable margarine
crystallized ginger, to
decorate

MAKES ABOUT 12 OZ

Knead the fondant until pliable, gradually working in the ginger syrup. Roll out the fondant to about ½ inch thick on a board lightly dusted with confectioners' sugar. Cut out shapes, using the same cutter each time. Leave the fondants to dry on parchment paper.

When the centers are thoroughly dry, break the chocolate into a bowl and melt it over a pan of hot water. Add a little margarine if necessary to achieve a dipping consistency.

Using a dipping ring, dip the ginger creams one at a time in the chocolate to give them a generous coating. Place on parchment. Before the chocolate dries, place a tiny sliver of crystallized ginger in the center of each one. Leave to dry.

Chocolate Coffee Creams

Different brands of coffee extracts may vary in their strength of flavor. Add only a few drops of extract to begin with, then taste the fondant and if not strong enough add a little more.

½ lb (1 cup) basic fondant (see page 42)
2 teaspoons heavy cream
few drops of coffee extract
few drops of brown food coloring

7 oz semi-sweet chocolate
about ½ tablespoon vegetable margarine

MAKES ABOUT 12 OZ

Knead the fondant until pliable, gradually working in the cream, coffee extract to taste and a little brown coloring if necessary. Roll out the fondant to about ½ inch thick on a board lightly dusted with confectioners' sugar. Cut out shapes, using the same cutter each time. Leave the fondants to dry on parchment paper.

When the centers are thoroughly dry, break the chocolate into a bowl and melt it over a pan of hot water. Add a little margarine if necessary to achieve a dipping consistency.

Using a dipping ring, dip the coffee creams one at a time in the chocolate to give them a generous coating. Place on parchment. Before the chocolate dries, dip the tip of a skewer in the melted chocolate and lightly trail a line across each chocolate to decorate. Leave to dry.

Chocolate Cherry Creams

Try to keep the decorations on one type of center all the same – it is a means of identification and looks more professional than random decorating.

½ lb (1 cup) basic fondant (see page 42)
2 teaspoons cherry brandy
7 oz semi-sweet chocolate

about ½ tablespoon vegetable margarine
1 oz milk chocolate

MAKES ABOUT 12 OZ

Knead the fondant until pliable, gradually working in the cherry brandy. Roll out the fondant to about ½ inch thick on a board lightly dusted with confectioners' sugar. Cut into shapes, using the same cutter each time. Leave the fondants to dry on parchment paper.

When the centers are thoroughly dry, break the chocolate into a bowl and melt it over a pan of hot water. Add a little margarine if necessary to achieve a dipping consistency.

Using a dipping ring, dip the liqueur fondants one at a time in the chocolate to give them a generous coating. Place on parchment. When the chocolate is set, melt the milk chocolate in a bowl over hot water, thinning if necessary with a little margarine. Using the tip of a skewer, decorate the chocolates with a squiggle of milk chocolate. Leave to dry again.

CHOCOLATE DIPPED ORANGE PEEL (page 28)

Chocolate Hazelnut Clusters

These chocolates become favorites with everyone who tries them, and they are simple to make: just add the toasted whole hazelnuts to melted chocolate, then take out four nuts per cluster and leave to dry.

½ lb (1½ cups) hazelnuts	about ½ tablespoon
8 oz semi-sweet chocolate	vegetable margarine

MAKES ABOUT 12 OZ

Spread the hazelnuts on a baking sheet. Toast in a preheated 350° oven for about 10 minutes, turning them or shaking the tray from time to time. Put the nuts into a clean dish towel and rub off the skins. Leave the nuts to cool.

Break the chocolate into a bowl and melt it over a pan of hot water. Add a little margarine if necessary to achieve a coating consistency.

Remove the pan from the heat, drop in the nuts and stir them around. Using a teaspoon, retrieve four nuts at a time with a good portion of chocolate. Place them in a little heap on parchment. If the chocolate starts to cool and thicken while making the clusters, return the pan to the heat but take care not to overheat the chocolate or it will become too runny to work with. Leave the hazelnut clusters to dry thoroughly.

Chocolate Dipped Fresh Fruit

For these chocolates, choose a fairly firm fruit that does not perish too easily, and one that will not discolor when peeled. Oranges, tangerines and pineapple are ideal, peaches and nectarines are good, and strawberries are delicious if good firm ones are chosen. Do not try to dip raspberries as they will collapse too quickly, and pears or apples are unsuitable as they rapidly turn brown. I have suggested macerating the fruit in Kirsch, but you could choose another liqueur such as Grand Marnier or brandy. These chocolates are best eaten the same day, so they make a good present to take with you to a dinner party. For a more enduring confection, use the same method to dip candied fruit (see page 92).

1 lb fresh fruit	about ½ tablespoon
¼ cup Kirsch	vegetable margarine
1 lb semi-sweet or candy-making chocolate	

To prepare the fruit, remove any skin or peel. Remove all the pith and membrane from oranges; cut pineapple into rings and then into wedges; cut peaches and nectarines into quarters or slices. Strawberries look pretty with the hulls left in.

Lay the prepared fruit in a shallow dish and spoon the Kirsch over. Leave for 2–3 hours, turning the fruit from time to time. Take the fruit out of the liqueur and dry carefully on paper towels.

Break the chocolate into a bowl and melt it over a pan of hot water. Add a little margarine if necessary to achieve a dipping consistency.

Remove the pan from the heat while you work; keep stirring the chocolate from time to time to keep it evenly melted. If it starts to thicken too much, reheat the water gently until the chocolate is back up to temperature. Put a sheet of parchment beside the pan ready to receive the dipped fruits.

You can either dip the fruit completely in the chocolate, using a dipping fork, or half dip it, holding one end of the fruit in your fingers – it looks pretty and very effective half dipped. Strawberries, even if completely dipped, should be held by the leaves to prevent those becoming coated in chocolate. The surface of the fruit must be completely dry when you dip it, or the moisture will spoil the chocolate. To coat completely, drop a piece of fruit into the chocolate, push it under the surface with a dipping fork then lift out. Hold the coated fruit over the bowl for a moment to drain, then wipe a skewer gently underneath the fork to remove any surplus chocolate. Carefully slide the fruit off the fork onto the parchment. Gently push the fruit very slightly with the fork to seal the chocolate underneath.

Leave until completely dry before removing from the paper, handling them as little as possible.

Dipped Apricot Rounds

To achieve a really dry apricot paste, you must simmer the apricots very slowly – a heat diffuser will help. The result is well worth the trouble as the fruity flavor is delicious.

½ lb (1⅓ cups) dried apricots	1½–2 tablespoons blanched almonds
¼ cup water	
⅓ cup sugar	MAKES ABOUT ½ lb
6 oz semi-sweet chocolate	

Mince or finely chop the apricots and put them in a saucepan with the water. Cover and simmer, stirring, for about 20 minutes until a thick paste forms. Stir in the sugar and simmer, stirring well, for a further 10 minutes, until quite dry. Remove from the heat and leave to cool.

When the apricot paste is cold, take a small piece at a time and roll into a ball. Place on parchment and flatten slightly.

Break the chocolate into a bowl and melt it over a pan of hot water. Using a dipping ring, dip the apricot rounds one at a time in the chocolate to give a generous coating. Place on parchment. Before the chocolate dries, decorate each one with an almond. Leave to dry.

Chocolate Walnut Creams

The soft, smooth, nutty paste provides a delightful contrast in texture to the walnut halves. The distinctive shape of the walnut under the chocolate means that no final decoration is needed.

½ lb (2 cups) walnut halves
⅔ cup sugar
½ lightly beaten egg
7 oz semi-sweet chocolate

about ½ tablespoon vegetable margarine

MAKES ABOUT 40

Grind half of the walnuts in a nut mill, blender or food processor. Mix the ground nuts and sugar in a bowl, then work in the egg to form a light paste. Knead the paste with your fingers until firm. Roll out the walnut paste to about ¼ inch thick on a board lightly dusted with confectioners' sugar. Cut into circles, using a 1 inch plain round cutter. Press a walnut half firmly into each circle of paste.

Break the chocolate into a bowl and melt it over a pan of hot water. Add a little margarine if necessary to achieve a dipping consistency.

Using a dipping ring, dip the walnut rounds one at a time into the chocolate to give them a generous coating. Place on parchment to dry.

Soft Almond Centers

Soft and nutty, these chocolates have an almond paste center and are decorated with flakes of toasted almonds. Toasting almonds takes only a few minutes yet enhances the flavor enormously.

3 tablespoons slivered almonds
¾ cup ground almonds
⅔ cup sugar
½ lightly beaten egg
7 oz semi-sweet chocolate

about ½ tablespoon vegetable margarine

MAKES ABOUT 40

Spread the slivered almonds on a baking sheet, toast lightly under a hot broiler for a few minutes or in a preheated 350° oven for about 5 minutes. Leave to cool.

Put the ground almonds and sugar in a bowl and work together with a fork, adding just enough egg to bind to a light paste. Knead the paste with your fingers until firm. Roll out the almond paste to about ¼ inch thick on a board lightly dusted with confectioners' sugar. With a sharp knife, cut into diamonds 1 inch long.

Break the chocolate into a bowl and melt it over a pan of hot water. Add a little margarine if necessary, to achieve a dipping consistency.

Using a dipping ring, dip the almond shapes one at a time in the chocolate to give them a generous coating. Place on parchment. Before the chocolate dries, place a flake of toasted almond in the center of each one.

Chocolate Brazils

Although it adds a little more work, freshly shelled nuts are always better than those you buy already shelled. Make sure all the brown skin is removed as well as the shell.

7 oz semi-sweet or milk chocolate
½ lb shelled Brazil nuts

about ½ tablespoon vegetable margarine

MAKES ABOUT 12 OZ

Break the chocolate into a bowl and melt it over a pan of hot water. Add a little margarine if necessary to achieve a dipping consistency.

Using a dipping ring, dip each nut in turn, rolling it briefly in the chocolate and lifting out quickly. Let the excess chocolate drain off, then place the coated nut on parchment. Leave to dry.

Chocolate Dipped Orange Peel

You can candy orange peel using the method given for fruit on page 92, but the method used in this recipe is much quicker and quite adequate for peel that is not going to be stored for long. Peel candied in this way can be stored for 2–3 months, but for use with chocolate it is nicest used when fresh.

3–4 oranges	8 oz semi-sweet chocolate
sugar	about ½ tablespoon
½ vanilla bean	vegetable margarine

Scrub the oranges, then carefully remove the peel in quarters. Cut the peel into strips about ¼ inch wide. Put the peel in a saucepan, cover with cold water and bring slowly to a boil. Drain off the water, cover with fresh cold water and bring to a boil again. Drain and repeat three more times, then drain and weigh or measure the cooked peel.

Return the peel to the pan and add 1 cup of sugar for each cup (6 oz) of peel. Add the vanilla bean and just cover with boiling water. Heat gently, stirring, until the sugar has dissolved. Bring to a boil and boil gently until the peel is tender and clear. Remove the pan from the heat and leave to cool.

Remove the peel from the syrup, draining well. Toss in sugar. Spread out the pieces on a wire rack and leave to dry. If after several hours it is still sticky, roll in sugar again. Do not store until completely dry.

To coat the peel, break the chocolate into a bowl and melt it over a pan of hot water. Add a little margarine if necessary to achieve a dipping consistency. With your fingers, break the surplus sugar off the peel.

Using a dipping fork, dip the candied peel, one piece at a time, in the chocolate as for fresh fruit.

Save a few pieces of peel undipped to pack with the chocolate ones – it adds a good color contrast to the selection in the box.

Noisettes

The centers for these popular chocolates are made from a hazelnut paste, each chocolate being topped with a chocolate coated whole hazelnut.

5 oz (1 cup) hazelnuts	about ½ tablespoon
⅔ cup sugar	vegetable margarine
½ lightly beaten egg	
8 oz semi-sweet chocolate	MAKES ABOUT 30

Spread the hazelnuts on a baking sheet. Lightly toast them under a hot broiler or in a preheated 400° oven for 5–10 minutes. Rub the nuts briskly in a dish towel to remove the skins. Grind ¾ cup of the nuts in a nut mill, blender or food processor, leaving the rest whole.

Mix the sugar with the ground nuts, then work to a paste with the beaten egg. Knead with your fingers until the paste is firm. Roll out to about ½ inch thick on a board lightly dusted with confectioners' sugar. Cut into 1-inch squares, using a cutter or sharp knife.

Break a third of the chocolate into a bowl and melt it over a pan of hot water. Add a little margarine to achieve a good coating consistency. Drop the whole hazelnuts into the melted chocolate and remove them, one at a time, with a dipping ring. Place on parchment and leave to dry.

Break the remaining chocolate into the melted chocolate and melt it over the hot water, adding a little more margarine if necessary to achieve a dipping consistency.

Dip the hazelnut paste centers, one at a time, in the chocolate to give them a generous coating. Place on parchment. Before the chocolate dries, put a coated hazelnut in the center of each one. Leave to dry.

Chocolate Raspberry Creams

Gum arabic is a resin taken from the acacia tree and is used as a setting agent; it is generally obtainable from specialty shops. These mouth-watering raspberry centers are very soft.

4 cups confectioners' sugar	8 oz candy-making chocolate
½ oz gum arabic	crystallized rose petals
5 tablespoons cold water	
raspberry extract	MAKES ABOUT 40
red food coloring	

Sift the confectioners' sugar onto a piece of wax paper. Sprinkle the gum arabic over the water in a small bowl and leave to soak until softened. Place the bowl in a pan of hot water and stir until dissolved. If necessary, strain it through a cheesecloth-lined sieve into a larger bowl.

Mix in enough of the sifted confectioners' sugar to form a mixture of piping consistency. Blend in a few drops of raspberry extract and tint very lightly to a pale pink with the red food coloring.

Using a pastry bag and ½-inch plain tube, pipe small lengths onto parchment. Leave to dry overnight, turning them when it is possible to lift them off the paper.

Break the chocolate into a bowl and melt it over a pan of hot water. Using a dipping fork, dip the raspberry centers, one at a time, into the chocolate to give a generous coating. Place on parchment. Before the chocolate dries, decorate with crystallized rose petals. Leave to set.

Chocolate Mint Crisps

These very smooth chocolate squares or diamonds, studded with tiny pieces of crisp peppermint caramel, are the perfect accompaniments to after-dinner coffee.

⅓ cup sugar
¼ cup water
oil of peppermint
8 oz semi-sweet chocolate
½ tablespoon vegetable
 margarine

5 tablespoons heavy
 cream

MAKES ABOUT 12 OZ

Oil a baking sheet. Line a small cake pan, about 6 inches square, or a 9×4 inch foil dish, with parchment.

Put the sugar and water in a small, heavy saucepan and heat very gently until the sugar has dissolved, stirring continuously. Bring to a boil, without stirring. Add 2–3 drops of oil of peppermint and boil the syrup rapidly to a rich brown caramel. Pour it onto the prepared baking sheet and leave to harden. When the caramel is really hard, crush roughly with a rolling pin.

Break the chocolate into a bowl and melt it over a pan of hot water. Add a little margarine to make it really smooth. Remove from the heat.

Put the cream in a small pan and bring to a boil. Pour onto the melted chocolate and beat until well mixed. Add the crushed peppermint caramel and beat for 2 minutes more, until the chocolate mixture is really smooth and the caramel evenly distributed. Turn the mixture into the prepared pan and smooth the surface. Leave overnight until firm.

Turn out the slab of mint chocolate onto a board and peel off the parchment. Dust a sharp knife with sweetened cocoa powder and carefully cut the chocolate mint crisp into square or diamond shapes.

CHOCOLATE MINT CRISPS (above)

Coffee Ganache

———◆◆◆———

Ganache is a sort of custard, but is so thick that it sets firmly enough to dip. Because of the cream, these deliciously large chocolates only keep a few days.

1 egg yolk	about ½ tablespoon
3 tablespoons sugar	vegetable margarine
½ cup heavy cream	
15 oz semi-sweet	MAKES 14
chocolate	
coffee extract	

Put the egg yolk in a bowl and stir in the sugar until well mixed. Add the cream and blend thoroughly together. Place the bowl over a pan of hot water and cook gently, stirring continuously, until the custard thickens enough to coat the back of a spoon. Remove from the heat and leave to cool.

Break 8 oz of the chocolate into a bowl and melt it over a pan of hot water. When really soft, remove from the heat and stir in the cooled custard. Add coffee extract to taste. Beat until smooth. Leave to cool until stiff enough to pipe.

Using a pastry bag and ½-inch star tube, pipe whirls of ganache onto parchment, making them about 1 inch across. Alternatively, form the custard into egg shapes, using two teaspoons. Put the centers in the refrigerator to harden.

When they are firm enough to handle, break the remaining chocolate into a bowl and melt it over a pan of hot water. Add a little margarine if necessary to achieve a dipping consistency.

Using a dipping ring, dip the centers one at a time in the chocolate to give them a generous coating. Place on parchment. Leave to dry.

———◆◆◆———

Dipped Orange Ganache

———◆◆◆———

These irresistible orange flavored set custard centers look especially pretty decorated with home-made candied orange peel (see page 28).

1 egg yolk	about ½ tablespoon
3 tablespoons sugar	vegetable margarine
½ cup heavy cream	candied orange peel, to
15 oz semi-sweet	decorate
chocolate	
few drops of orange	MAKES ABOUT 24
extract	

Put the egg yolk in a bowl and stir in the sugar until well mixed. Add the cream and blend thoroughly together. Place the bowl over a pan of hot water and cook gently, stirring continuously, until the custard thickens enough to coat the back of a spoon. Remove from the heat and leave to cool.

Break 8 oz of the chocolate into a bowl and melt it over a pan of hot water. When really soft, remove from the heat and stir in the cooled custard. Add orange extract to taste. Beat until smooth. Leave to cool until stiff enough to pipe.

Using a pastry bag and ½-inch star tube, pipe the ganache into lengths of about 1¼ inches onto parchment. Put the centers in the refrigerator to set.

When they are firm enough to handle, break the remaining chocolate into a bowl and melt it over a pan of hot water. Add a little margarine if necessary to achieve a dipping consistency. Using a dipping fork and holding the centers lengthwise, dip them one at a time in the chocolate to give them a generous coating. Place on parchment. Before the chocolate dries, decorate with tiny pieces of candied orange peel. Leave to dry.

Solid Chocolate Eggs

Like all chocolates, these become dull if exposed to the air for long, so wrap them in foil or plastic wrap if they are to be kept for more than a day or two.

4 eggs	crystallized violets
1 lb semi-sweet or milk chocolate	crystallized rose petals

If you have never blown an egg before, now is the time to try. With a needle, pierce a tiny hole in each end of one of the eggs and blow out the contents. Enlarge the hole in one end to take a small pastry tube and wash out the shell with cold water. Leave to dry thoroughly while you blow the rest of the eggs. (Drying will be accelerated by putting the eggs on a radiator.) When they are dry, put a piece of tape over the small hole in each egg so that it cannot leak.

Break the chocolate into a bowl and melt it over a pan of hot water, stirring well. When it reaches pouring consistency, spoon into a pastry bag fitted with a small tube and pipe into the egg shells through the large hole. Swirl it around from time to time to remove any air bubbles. Leave the eggs overnight to set.

Carefully crack the eggs and peel off the shells. Decorate the solid chocolate eggs with crystallized violets, rose petals and narrow ribbons, sticking them on with melted chocolate. Alternatively, wrap each egg tightly in colored foil. Place them in egg cups or arrange in a basket.

Chocolate Marshmallows

*If you find this marshmallow too difficult to handle, you could increase the quantity of gelatin; but it tastes **much** nicer if only lightly set.*

oil, cornstarch and
   confectioners' sugar,
   for coating pan
1⅔ cups sugar
⅔ cup water
6 teaspoons unflavored
   gelatin
1 teaspoon rose water

red food coloring
1 egg white
sweetened cocoa powder

MAKES ABOUT 1 lb

Oil a 7-inch-square baking pan and line the bottom with wax paper. Oil the paper and dredge with a mixture of a little sifted cornstarch and confectioners' sugar.

Put the sugar and ¼ pint water in a heavy saucepan and heat gently, stirring, until the sugar has completely dissolved. Boil steadily to 260°, without stirring the syrup.

Meanwhile, sprinkle the gelatin over 3 tablespoons water in a heatproof measuring cup and leave to soften a little. Place the cup in a pan of hot water and dissolve the gelatin completely. Add enough water to make ⅔ cup and pour into a bowl.

When the syrup reaches 260°, pour it onto the dissolved gelatin. Add the rose water and a few drops of red food coloring, then beat. Add the egg white and continue beating until the mixture is thick enough to hold its shape. Pour into the prepared pan and smooth the top. Leave to set overnight.

When the marshmallow is set, turn it onto a board dusted with cocoa powder. Cut into 1-inch strips, then down into ¼–½-inch slices. Roll each piece in sifted cocoa powder and arrange in a box, overlapping one piece slightly on the next.

CHOCOLATE EASTER EGG (page 38)

Brandy Cream Cups

For these chocolate cups, foil bonbon cases or two paper cases, one inside the other, are the most suitable to use.

9 oz candy-making chocolate	1 tablespoon butter brandy extract
8 oz semi-sweet chocolate	
½ cup heavy cream	MAKES ABOUT 24

Break the candy-making chocolate into a bowl and melt it over a pan of hot water. Spoon a small amount of the melted chocolate into a foil bonbon case or two paper cases, using one inside the other. Swirl the chocolate around until the case is well coated. Leave to dry upside down on parchment. Repeat, making about 24 chocolate cups.

When dry, coat the molds with a second layer if the first looks thin. Leave to set thoroughly. Set the remaining chocolate aside.

Grate the semi-sweet chocolate. Put the cream in a small, heavy saucepan and very slowly bring to a boil. Add the grated chocolate and stir over the heat until melted. Whisk in the butter and brandy extract to taste. Leave to cool.

Spoon a little of the cold brandy cream into each chocolate cup and smooth the tops. Reheat the candy-making chocolate again until it runs. Spoon a little chocolate over each cup, smoothing it over and shaking from side to side so that it floods right to the edges. Leave to set.

When the tops are thoroughly dry, peel off the cases and place the chocolate cups in fresh bonbon cases.

Walnut Cups

The crunchy, nutty texture provides a pleasing surprise in these chocolate cups. The filling is like a praline but made with walnuts mixed with chocolate.

10 oz candy-making chocolate	1 tablespoon water
2 oz (½ cup) walnut halves	2 oz semi-sweet chocolate
⅓ cup sugar	MAKES ABOUT 30

Break the candy-making chocolate into a bowl and melt it over a pan of hot water. Using foil bonbon cases or double paper cases as molds, spoon a little chocolate into each case and swirl it around to coat. Leave to dry upside down on parchment. Repeat, making about 30 chocolate cups. Apply a second coat if the first one looks thin. Leave to set thoroughly. Set the remaining chocolate aside.

Grind the walnuts in a nut mill, blender or food processor. Put the sugar and water in a small, heavy saucepan and heat gently, stirring, until the sugar has completely dissolved. Bring to a boil and boil for 1–2 minutes, without stirring. Remove from the heat, stir in the ground walnuts and set aside.

Break the semi-sweet chocolate into a bowl and melt it over a pan of hot water. When the nut mixture and the melted chocolate are about the same temperature, stir them together. Leave to cool before filling the chocolate cups.

Spoon a little of the nut mixture into the chocolate cups and smooth the tops. Reheat the candy-making chocolate until it runs again. Flood the tops of the cups, covering the filling completely to the edges.

Before the chocolate dries, decorate each one with a small piece of walnut. Leave to set.

When the tops are thoroughly dry, peel off the cases and place the chocolate cups in fresh bonbon cases.

Rum and Raisin Cups

There is a superb surprise filling of cake and raisins soaked in rum when you bite into these chocolates. They make a perfect Christmas gift.

10 oz candy-making chocolate	½ cup rum
2¼ cups stale sponge cake crumbs	extra raisins, to decorate
scant ½ cup raisins	MAKES ABOUT 30

Break the chocolate into a bowl and melt it over a pan of hot water. Using foil bonbon cases or double paper cases as molds, spoon a little chocolate into each case and swirl it around to coat. Leave to dry upside down on parchment. Repeat, making about 30 chocolate cups. Apply a second coat if the first one looks thin. Leave to set thoroughly.

Meanwhile, put the sponge cake crumbs into a small bowl and mix in the raisins. Cover with rum and leave until the liquid is soaked up.

Spoon a little of the soaked cake and raisin mixture into the chocolate cups. Reheat the chocolate until it runs again. Flood the tops of the cups, covering the filling completely to the edges. Before the chocolate dries, place an unsoaked raisin in the center of each one. Leave to set.

When the tops are thoroughly dry, peel off the cases and place the chocolate cups in fresh bonbon cases.

Chocolate Praline

The crunchy praline chocolate centers make a good contrast to the smooth chocolate coating. Crystallized violets make pretty decorations, but if you prefer to keep to nuts, top each chocolate with a sliver of toasted almond.

3 oz (⅔ cup) unblanched almonds	7 oz candy-making chocolate
½ cup sugar	crystallized violets or toasted slivered almonds, to decorate
7 oz semi-sweet chocolate	
	MAKES ABOUT 1 lb

Oil a baking sheet. Put the almonds and sugar in a small, heavy saucepan and heat very gently until the sugar has dissolved, stirring to prevent the sugar from sticking to the pan. Continue to heat until the sugar caramelizes to a light golden color and the nuts are lightly toasted. Pour the mixture onto the prepared baking sheet and leave to set. When completely hard, finely crush the praline with a rolling pin or grind in a nut mill.

Break the semi-sweet chocolate into a bowl and melt it over a pan of hot water. Mix in the praline to make a stiff paste and turn it into a 7-inch-square pan. Leave to set.

Cut the chocolate praline into squares. Break the candy-making chocolate into a bowl and melt it over a pan of hot water. Using a dipping ring, dip the chocolate praline, one piece at a time, into the chocolate to give a generous coating. Before the coating dries, decorate each square with a piece of crystallized violet. Leave to dry.

Chocolate Easter Egg

Buy a mold or a hollow chocolate shell from speciality cook shops or by mail from manufacturers of specialist plastic goods – those who make products for the freezer and microwave usually also make molds suitable for chocolate work. The amount of chocolate to use is not given as sizes of different manufacturer's molds vary.

Break the chocolate into a bowl and melt it over a pan of hot water. Make sure the bowl does not touch the water, and that the water does not boil. Heat gently until the chocolate melts, stirring gently from time to time. It is ready to use at about 85°, when it should be completely melted but quite thick. Add a little margarine if necessary so that the chocolate runs freely.

Remove the bowl from the heat, so that the chocolate does not continue getting hotter, and pour a little into the mold. Tilt and swirl it around until the whole surface is well coated, adding more chocolate as necessary. Place the mold, open side down, on parchment and leave to dry. When dry, you will be able to see if there are any thin areas. If so, melt some more chocolate and add another layer.

When the chocolate is thoroughly set, it should start to shrink away from the side of the mold. Ease off the mold, then make the second half of the shell (it is quicker to buy two chocolate egg molds, of course).

Fill one half of the shell with chocolates or other candies, then fill the top half with crumpled parchment, to prevent them from being damaged. Stick the halves together either by brushing the seam with a little melted chocolate, or by piping decoratively around the seam.

Decorate the egg with marzipan flowers or ornamental Easter chicks, ice a name on or add pre-made decorations such as crystallized violets or silk flowers, depending on whether you are making for a child or an adult. Stick the decorations on with little dabs of melted chocolate. Tie a ribbon around to hold the egg securely together.

VANILLA CREAM FONDANTS (page 44)

Fondants

FONDANTS are the epitome of confectionery work. Smooth, sugar morsels, meltingly soft in texture, fine and delicate in flavor, they are also exquisitely pretty to look at. Whether your gift is a box of mixed fondants, or a selection of different types of candies, the fondants sparkle invitingly, just waiting to be eaten.

Fondant work is somewhat more exacting than other branches of candy-making. Not only is the precise temperature of the boiling syrup important, but so is the working of the syrup into the characteristic, soft texture. The syrup has to be "turned" with a spatula and then kneaded by hand until fine, even crystals form in a soft and workable mass. The fondant is also best matured for several days before use – it is possible to shape it immediately but much easier and more successful if you wrap the fondant in an airtight package and let it rest. So a gift of fondants is not a spur-of-the-moment affair; a little planning is required to accommodate the different stages.

When making a basic fondant mixture, add some of the sugar in the form of corn syrup. This will encourage the formation of fine, even-sized crystals instead of large, coarse ones. Then follow the usual rules for sugar boiling (see page 13). Stir the syrup over a very low heat until the sugar has dissolved and there is absolutely no trace of undissolved sugar; on no account let it boil. If necessary use a heat diffuser to achieve the low, even heat required.

Then boil rapidly, without stirring, to the temperature stated in the recipe. If you stir during this boiling, it will encourage the formation of the rough crystals that you do not want.

Have a cold baking sheet or marble slab ready for turning the fondant. Traditionally a marble slab was used, but if you are making more than about ½ pound of fondant you will need a very large slab indeed to hold the syrup. Also, since boiling sugar syrup is dangerously hot, better be safe than sorry and use a baking sheet with sides about 1 inch deep to contain it within bounds. The important factors are that the surface should be really cold and that you should have room to work – which is why a bowl is not ideal.

There are two basic methods of shaping the final candies. Either you can re-melt the fondant, flavor and color it and pour it into molds. Or you can knead the fondant, roll it out and cut it with fancy cutters. The first method produces a candy with a slightly finer, smoother texture; use a plastic sheet of molds, flexible enough to allow you to turn out the finished fondants without damaging them.

To knead and cut the fondant, you need to work in a cool, dry atmosphere. A hot or humid kitchen, even hot lights, makes the fondant too hot to shape. Sometimes even the warmth of your hands will make it too soft by the time you have added liquid flavorings. If this happens, tightly cover the surface of the fondant with plastic wrap, then place in the refrigerator overnight to firm up again. Alternatively, sift in a little extra confectioners' sugar. However if the fondant is too hard, knead in a little syrup stock (see page 42).

At the end of this chapter there are a few recipes for uncooked creams. These are not true fondants, but they are pleasant candies that are quickly made. Many people will choose to use them for that reason. They are also ideal if children want to be involved in the making – boiling sugar is dangerous with children around. The uncooked creams do not keep well, so should be eaten within two to three days.

Basic Fondant

Traditionally, fondant is worked on a marble slab but for this large quantity that is not really practical, even if you have one. You need a wide baking sheet or tray with deep enough edges to contain the hot syrup; I use the large deep baking sheet supplied with my oven; an alternative might be a large stainless steel mixing bowl.

3 lb (8 cups) sugar
2 cups water

4 tablespoons light corn syrup

MAKES ABOUT 3 lbs

Put the sugar, water and corn syrup in a saucepan and dissolve the sugar slowly over a low heat, stirring all the time. When the sugar is completely dissolved, bring the syrup slowly to a boil. Boil to 240°, without stirring. Remove from the heat and leave until all the bubbles have disappeared from the surface.

Sprinkle a little water on a baking sheet and pour the syrup onto it. As the syrup touches the cold, damp surface, it will start to thicken. Leave to cool until a skin starts to form around the edges.

Using a wooden spatula, draw the edges into the center and work the mixture in a figure-eight movement. It will gradually shrink into a hard, crystalline white lump. Once this is achieved, scrape the fondant off the sheet and knead with your hands until smooth and even textured, soft and pliable.

If possible, the fondant should be left for two to three days before use; in fact, it will keep for

up to six weeks if necessary – which is why it is worth making a large quantity at once. Put the fondant in a plastic container with an airtight lid, cover the surface closely with plastic wrap and seal the lid on tightly. The plastic wrap prevents the surface from drying out – if the surface does harden it will spoil the fondant. In hot weather, keep the fondant in the refrigerator.

When you take out part of the fondant for use, be sure to press the plastic wrap down over the surface again to keep out the air, and to re-seal the box tightly.

Syrup Stock

Use this syrup to adjust the texture of basic fondant that has hardened during storage. The syrup will keep for four to six weeks.

1½ cups sugar
⅔ cup water

Put the sugar and water in a saucepan and heat gently, stirring until the sugar is dissolved. Bring to a boil and boil without stirring again to 216°, a thick syrup. Leave to cool. Strain the cooled syrup through a cheesecloth-lined sieve to remove any possible sugar.

left TUTTI FRUTTI CREAMS (page 49);
bottom PEPPERMINT CREAMS (page 49)

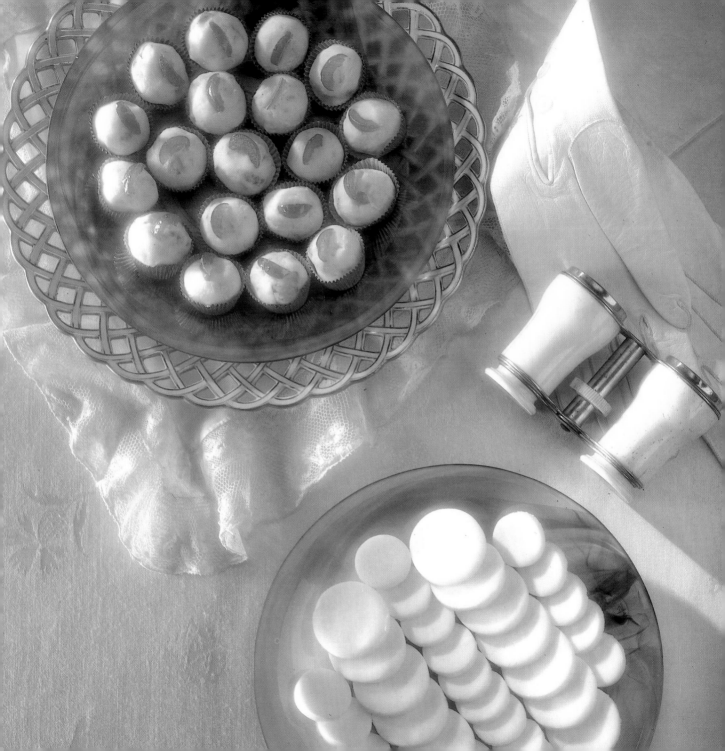

Vanilla Cream Fondants

Plain, simple, creamy-flavored confections, these make a good contrast to a selection of dark chocolates. There are two methods here for shaping the fondant, either in molds or by rolling out and cutting shapes.

½ lb (1 cup) basic fondant
  (see page 42)
2 teaspoons heavy cream
syrup stock (see page 42)
few drops of vanilla
  extract

Decoration
silver balls
crystallized violets

MAKES ABOUT ½ lb

◆ *Using fondant molds* ◆

Put the fondant into a bowl over a saucepan of hot water and let it melt. The bowl should not touch the water and the water should not boil.

Stir in the heavy cream until well blended. If necessary, add a little of the syrup stock – you need only enough syrup to make the fondant pourable, and you may need none at all. When the fondant is of a pouring consistency, remove the bowl from the heat and dry the bottom carefully so that no drops of water drip into the mixture while you are working. Stir in a few drops of vanilla extract.

Carefully spoon or pour the fondant into a sheet of molds and leave to set and harden. They should be hard enough to turn out in about 4 hours, but they may be better left a little longer before you handle them much.

Gently press two or three silver balls or a crystallized violet into the top of some of them. Place in paper bonbon cases.

◆ *Shaping with cutters* ◆

If you have no molds, you will have to knead in the cream and flavoring, a little at a time. If the fondant is too hard to handle, add a little syrup; if it is too soft, sift a very little confectioners' sugar over it – no more than 1 teaspoon – and knead in. Chilling for a while in the refrigerator also helps to make fondant firmer.

When the flavorings are well blended in and the fondant is pliable, roll out to about ½ inch thick on a board lightly dusted with confectioners' sugar. Cut into shapes with a fancy petit four or candy cutter and press the decorations on top immediately. Leave until the outsides have hardened before putting them into paper bonbon cases.

Fondants Crème de Menthe

The crème de menthe gives these fondants a delicate pale green tint as well as a delicious minty flavor.

½ lb (1 cup) basic fondant (see page 42)	**syrup stock (see page 42)**
a little heavy cream	MAKES ½ lb
1–2 teaspoons crème de menthe liqueur	

Melt the fondant in a bowl over a pan of hot water, as for Vanilla Cream Fondants (see page 44). Stir in the cream and crème de menthe. If necessary to make it pourable, add a little syrup stock.

Carefully spoon or pour the mixture into the fondant molds and leave to set and harden. Turn out the fondants and place in paper bonbon cases.

Black Currant Cream Fondants

½ lb (1 cup) basic fondant (see page 42)	**crystallized rose petals, to decorate**
1 teaspoon heavy cream	MAKES ½ lb
1–2 teaspoons black currant or blackberry syrup	

Knead the fondant by hand until it starts to soften. Knead in the cream and black currant syrup, a little

at a time, to achieve a soft, pliable mixture.

Roll out the fondant on a board lightly dusted with confectioners' sugar. Cut into shapes about ½ inch thick with a fancy petit four or candy cutter and decorate with crystallized rose petals. Leave until set and hardened, then place in paper bonbon cases.

Alternatively, melt the fondant, add the cream and flavoring, then pour into molds as for Vanilla Cream Fondants (see page 44).

Ginger Fondants

When the basic fondant is used for coating, it goes crisp and shiny. Ginger fondants are delicious – hot-flavored but sweet, crisp on the outside, softer in the center. Use a good-quality crystallized ginger, not the type sold specifically for baking which usually has less flavor. Or, for a really hot confection, try preserved ginger, drying it well before dipping.

1 lb (2 cups) basic fondant (see page 42)	**½ lb crystallized ginger pieces**
syrup from a jar of preserved ginger	MAKES ABOUT 1 lb

Melt the fondant in a bowl over a pan of hot water. Thin the fondant with a little syrup from a jar of preserved ginger – it should lightly coat the back of a wooden spoon.

Using a dipping ring, dip the pieces of ginger one at a time into the fondant. Lift out, drain for a moment and place on a wire rack to dry.

Fondants Framboises

Framboise liqueur has a pronounced flavor, producing distinctive raspberry fondants.

½ lb (1 cup) basic fondant (see page 42)
2 teaspoons heavy cream
1–2 drops pink food coloring

1–2 teaspoons framboise liqueur

MAKES ½ lb

Melt the fondant in a bowl over a pan of hot water, as for Vanilla Cream Fondants (see page 44). Stir in the cream. Add pink food coloring to tint the mixture a very pale pink. Remove from the heat and gently stir in the liqueur. Pour into the fondant molds and leave to set and harden. Turn out the fondants and place in paper bonbon cases.

If you are shaping the fondant by rolling out and using cutters (see Vanilla Cream Fondants), you will have to knead in the coloring very thoroughly by hand or it will be streaky.

Drambuie Fondants

Whiskey-based Drambuie liqueur is an excellent flavoring for fondants.

½ lb (1 cup) basic fondant (see page 42)
2 teaspoons heavy cream
2 teaspoons Drambuie

MAKES ½ lb

Knead the fondant by hand until it starts to soften. Knead in the cream and liqueur, a little at a time, to achieve a soft, pliable mixture.

Roll out the fondant to about ½ inch thick on a board lightly dusted with confectioners' sugar. Cut into shapes, using a petit four or candy cutter. Leave the fondants to set and harden, then place in paper bonbon cases.

Fondant Dates

These popular date sweetmeats, filled with almond-flavored fondant, are easy to make. Use the almond extract sparingly to avoid an overpowering flavor.

½ lb dried dates
½ lb (1 cup) basic fondant (see page 42)
1–2 drops almond extract

¼ cup chopped almonds, toasted
sugar, for rolling

MAKES 1 lb

Slit the dates lengthwise to remove the pits, leaving the two halves attached.

Knead the fondant until pliable, then knead in the almond extract and chopped nuts until evenly distributed.

Break off a small piece of fondant at a time, roll it into an oval and use to fill the centers of the dates.

Roll the fondant dates in sugar. Leave to dry, then place in paper bonbon cases.

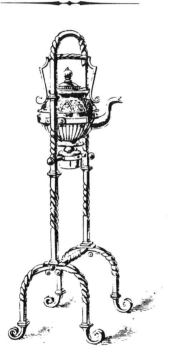

Pistachio Fondants

The nuts in this recipe take the edge off the sweetness – which some people prefer. Pistachio nuts have a green kernel covered by a thin reddish skin and are enclosed in a white shell. Here, the shelled nuts are blanched to reveal the attractive green kernel.

½ lb (1 cup) basic fondant (see page 42)	1 oz (⅓ cup) shelled pistachios
syrup stock (see page 42)	
few drops of green food coloring	MAKES ½ lb

Blanch the pistachios in a bowl of boiling water for about 10 minutes, then rub off the skins. Chop the nuts finely, reserving a few whole nuts for decoration.

Melt the fondant in a bowl over a pan of hot water, as for Vanilla Cream Fondants (see page 44). Soften if necessary with a little syrup and lightly tint with a few drops of green food coloring. Remove from the heat and stir in the chopped nuts. Pour into the fondant molds and leave to set and harden.

Turn out the fondants and decorate each one with a halved pistachio. Place in paper bonbon cases.

If you prefer to make all the fondants of one flavor in the same shape, you will have to knead in the coloring and nuts, then shape the fondant by rolling out and using a cutter.

Dipped Almond Fondants

*The many layers are inclined to make this candy
very large indeed. Keep the inner layer of
amaretto fondant as thin as you can.*

3 tablespoons blanched almonds	2⅔ cups sugar
½ lb (1 cup) basic fondant (see page 42)	1 cup water
1½ teaspoons amaretto liqueur	syrup stock (see page 42)
	MAKES ABOUT 1 lb

Dipping Fondant
tiny pinch of cream of
    tartar

Prepare the dipping fondant first so that it has a little time to mature before use. Stir the cream of tartar into a little cold water. Put the sugar and water in a saucepan and heat very gently, stirring, until the sugar has completely dissolved. Bring to a boil and add the cream of tartar. Boil to 236° and remove from the heat. This temperature, plus the addition of cream of tartar, will give a slightly softer fondant than the basic mixture.

Let the bubbles subside in the pan. Sprinkle a little water on a baking sheet and pour the syrup onto it. Leave to cool until a skin starts to form around the edges. Using a wooden spatula, work the fondant in a figure-eight movement until the sugar crystallizes and hardens, then knead by hand until soft and pliable (see page 44). Let stand while making the centers.

Spread the almonds on a baking sheet. Toast them lightly under the broiler or in a preheated 400° oven for about 10 minutes, shaking and turning them until lightly browned all over. Leave to cool.

Knead the basic fondant, working in the liqueur, until it is soft enough to mold. Break off a small piece at a time and place a toasted almond in the center. Roll up the fondant around the nut and form into a sphere between the palms of your hands. Leave to dry on parchment until well crusted, turning them so that they harden underneath too.

When the centers are dry, melt the dipping fondant in a bowl over a pan of hot water. Heat gently, stirring all the time, until just below boiling point. Add a little syrup stock if necessary to achieve a dipping consistency. Adjust the heat to keep the fondant at the same temperature, and continue to stir frequently while you work, to prevent a crust forming. Place a sheet of parchment near the pan.

Using a dipping ring, dip the almond centers, one at a time, into the fondant. Turn over quickly and lift out. Drain for a moment and, as you draw the ring aside, wipe it across the edge of the pan to remove any excess, but without touching the candy itself. Place the dipped almonds on the parchment to dry. (Remember to keep stirring the dipping fondant as you coat the candies.)

Leave to dry, then place carefully in paper bonbon cases.

Tutti Frutti Creams

Less delicate in texture and flavor than true fondants, these do have the advantage of being quick to make.

6 tablespoons heavy cream
6 cups confectioners' sugar
2 tablespoons very finely chopped mixed candied peel
3 tablespoons chopped glacé cherries

3 tablespoons chopped almonds
juice of ½ lemon
quartered glacé cherries, to decorate

MAKES ABOUT 1¼ lb

Put the cream in a large bowl and sift in the confectioners' sugar. Mix with a fork until well blended. Add the chopped peel, cherries, nuts and lemon juice. Knead well by hand until the fondant is smooth and the fruit and nuts well blended in.

Break off small pieces at a time and roll into small balls (dust your hands very lightly with confectioners' sugar if the mixture sticks). Flatten each ball slightly and press a piece of glacé cherry into the top of each one. Place in paper bonbon cases and leave to dry.

Peppermint Creams

Add peppermint extract sparingly as it is very strong! To really control how much you use, dip a toothpick into the bottle and shake the drops off the end of the toothpick.

1 small egg white
3 cups confectioners' sugar
1–2 drops oil of peppermint

MAKES ½ lb

Beat the egg white in a bowl until stiff. Sift in the confectioners' sugar and combine well to make a firm mixture. Carefully add the oil of peppermint to taste and blend in thoroughly.

Roll out the peppermint cream to about ¼ inch thick on a board lightly dusted with sifted confectioners' sugar. Cut into rounds, using a small round cutter. The trimmings can be kneaded together, rolled out again and used to make more peppermint creams. Leave to dry on a wire rack for about 12 hours. Pack in layers, with wax or parchment paper between the layers.

Sugar Mice

You can use the basic boiled fondant mixture to make mice by pouring it into a mold – certainly fondant made by the basic method keeps the best and the mice can be stored for some time. But if the children want to help make them, it is safer to avoid boiling sugar and make a simple mixture like this one. It is not as smooth and melty as the boiled one, but will still be very popular.

6 cups confectioners' sugar	silver balls
3 tablespoons light corn syrup	thin white string
1 egg white	MAKES ABOUT 24
various food colorings	

Sift the sugar into a bowl. Warm the syrup gently until it runs smoothly, then add to the sugar with the egg white. Mix well with a fork then knead by hand to make a smooth mixture.

Divide the mixture into three or four pieces. Leave one portion white and tint the others lightly with pink, yellow or green. Knead colorings in evenly.

Dust a board and your hands with sifted confectioner's sugar and shape the mixture into small mice, no more than about 2 inches long. For each one, make a small sausage shape, pointing it at the nose end. Cut a length of string, tie a knot in the end and press the knot into place under the mouse for a tail. For the ears, make two tiny balls, flatten and curve them and press in place. Use silver balls for eyes. Leave to dry.

Chocolate Creams

These do not have the delicacy of texture of a true fondant, but the flavor is good.

2 tablespoons evaporated milk	1 oz semi-sweet chocolate sweetened cocoa powder toasted almonds, to decorate
3 cups confectioners' sugar	
2 teaspoons brandy	MAKES ABOUT 10 OZ

Put the milk in a bowl and sift in the confectioners' sugar. Using a fork, gradually work together. Add the brandy and knead by hand until well blended.

Melt the chocolate in a small bowl over a pan of hot water. Leave to cool but not thicken. Add the melted chocolate to the brandy-flavored cream, scraping out the bowl well. Knead until the mixture is smooth and pliable.

Roll out the mixture to just over ¼ inch thick on a board very lightly dusted with cocoa powder. Cut into rounds, using a small round cutter. Decorate each one with a toasted almond. Leave to dry and harden, then place in paper bonbon cases.

SUGAR MICE (above)

Walnut Coffee Creams

These smooth, creamy, coffee-flavored fondants have a pleasing crunchy texture thanks to the walnut pieces.

2 tablespoons evaporated milk	3 cups confectioners' sugar
1 teaspoon Kahlua or Tia Maria	2 tablespoons chopped walnuts
3 drops coffee extract	walnut pieces, to decorate
few drops of brown food coloring	

MAKES ABOUT 8 OZ

Put the evaporated milk, liqueur, coffee extract and coloring in a bowl, then sift in the confectioners' sugar. Mix with a fork until the sugar is incorporated. Add the chopped nuts. Knead by hand until the fondant is smooth and pliable and the nuts are evenly distributed.

Roll out the fondant to about ½ inch thick on a board lightly dusted with confectioners' sugar. Cut into shapes, using petit four or candy cutters. Decorate each one with a piece of walnut. Leave to dry on a wire rack, then place in paper bonbon cases.

Tangerine Creams

If you don't believe that these will taste any different from orange creams – just try them. The creams are decorated with candied tangerine peel.

1 tangerine	finely grated rind of 2 tangerines
granulated sugar	3 cups confectioners' sugar
3 tablespoons heavy cream	orange food coloring

MAKES ABOUT 8 OZ

Scrub the whole tangerine and remove the peel in quarters. Use water and granulated sugar to candy the peel, using the method in Chocolate Dipped Orange Peel on page 28. Leave to dry.

Put the cream and grated rind in a bowl, then sift in the confectioners' sugar. Mix together with a fork. Knead by hand until smooth and pliable. Add a tiny amount of orange food coloring to lightly tint the fondant mixture.

Roll out the mixture to about ½ inch thick on a board lightly dusted with sifted confectioners' sugar. Cut out small shapes, using a fancy petit four or candy cutter.

Cut the candied peel into small diamonds or strips and use to decorate the candies. Leave to dry on a wire rack, then place in paper bonbon cases.

Fudge

FUDGE is probably the most popular home-made confectionery. I've never met anyone who didn't like it, and the home-made versions are usually better than mass-produced commercial ones. The finished product always has a slightly rough and ready look about it – you can't make fudge quite so glamorous and glossy as a box of chocolates. But the appeal is similar to that of a steaming stew in an earthen-ware casserole, compared to smoked salmon on a silver platter. The more homey one has a definite place in everybody's appetite.

Fudge keeps quite well, and the best place for home storage is in an airtight container. When the time comes to give the fudge away, pack it in layers between sheets of wax or baking parchment paper in a decorative box, or pile it into a glass jar. It is quite good-tempered and the pieces will not stick to each other, so there is no need for individual wrappings. If you are packing the fudge for sale at a bazaar, small plastic bags tied with ribbon are cheap yet pretty.

Fudge is basically a sugar syrup made with milk or cream. Its texture may be soft and creamy or crisp and grainy – tastes vary. I actually prefer the smoother textured fudges, but there are recipes for both kinds in this chapter.

As with all syrups, fudge must be stirred continually until the sugar is dissolved, and must not be allowed to boil until all crystals have disappeared. The point at which this is achieved is less obvious when the liquid is milk or cream as opposed to water, so do watch it carefully. If you stir with a metal spoon, you will be able to see any remaining sugar grains on the spoon. Then, as it boils, stir occasionally to prevent the milk from scorching on the bottom of the pan. If there is butter in the mixture, choose unsalted for preference as it burns less easily.

Adding a little honey or corn syrup makes a softer fudge – it converts some of the sugar to invert sugar which crystallizes into fine, even grains instead of large, coarse ones. The other factor which makes a big difference to the texture of fudge is beating it after it has finished boiling. If you beat the mixture while it is still very hot, it will grain quickly and set to a firm, rather granular, fudge. If you let it cool first and do not beat so much, the fudge will be softer and smoother. Try both to see which you prefer.

The usual temperature for making fudge is 240°, though you will find small variations on this in some of the recipes producing slightly different fudges.

Vanilla Fudge

This is a smooth, creamy fudge that makes a good base if you want to experiment with flavorings. It is less temperamental than those made with cream.

1½ lb (4 cups) sugar
6 tablespoons unsalted butter
scant 1 cup evaporated milk

scant 1 cup fresh milk
few drops of vanilla extract

MAKES ABOUT 2 lb

Oil a 7-inch-square baking pan. Put the sugar, butter and milks into a large, heavy pan and heat gently until the butter has melted and the sugar completely dissolved, stirring continuously. Turn up the heat and boil to 240°. Stir the mixture occasionally, to prevent the milk from burning on the bottom of the pan. As the mixture nears the correct temperature, lower the heat a little.

As soon as the temperature reaches 240°, remove from the heat and stir in the vanilla extract. Cool a little, then beat just until the mixture starts to leave a trail on itself.

Pour the fudge into the prepared pan. Let cool. Before the fudge hardens completely, mark into squares with a sharp knife. When completely cold and set, turn the fudge out and cut carefully into the marked squares.

Ginger Fudge

Make as for Vanilla Fudge, but omit the vanilla extract and beat in ½ cup chopped preserved ginger as soon as you remove the pan from the heat. Dry as much of the syrup off the ginger as you can, using paper towels, before you chop it. The result is one of the most popular fudges I make – the combination of hot and sweet flavors is a real winner.

VANILLA FUDGE (above); CHOCOLATE AND
HAZELNUT FUDGE (page 57)

Coconut Fudge

Toasting the coconut for this fudge helps to intensify the flavor.

5 tablespoons shredded coconut	2 tablespoons light corn syrup
1½ lb (4 cups) sugar	3 drops of vanilla extract
1 cup heavy cream	
	MAKES ABOUT 2 lb

Oil a 7-inch-square pan. Spread the coconut on a baking sheet. Lightly toast under the broiler or in a preheated 400° oven for about 5 minutes, shaking it from time to time and watching carefully to make sure the coconut doesn't scorch. Leave to cool.

Put the sugar, cream and corn syrup in a large, heavy saucepan and heat gently until the sugar has dissolved, stirring continuously. Bring to a boil and boil to 240°, stirring occasionally.

Remove the pan from the heat, wait for the bubbles to subside and stir in the vanilla extract and coconut. Cool a little, then beat until the mixture starts to leave a trail on itself.

Pour the fudge into the prepared pan. Leave to cool. Mark into squares as it begins to set. When completely cold and set, turn the fudge out and cut into the marked squares.

Coffee and Walnut Fudge

Coffee extracts vary. With mild ones, you will need to use about 2 tablespoons; with stronger varieties you will only need about 1 teaspoon.

1½ lb (4 cups) sugar	scant 1 cup fresh milk
6 tablespoons unsalted butter	coffee extract
scant 1 cup evaporated milk	½ cup chopped walnuts
	MAKES ABOUT 2 lb

Oil a 7-inch-square pan. Put the sugar, butter and milks in a large, heavy saucepan and heat gently until the sugar has dissolved, stirring continuously. Bring to a boil and boil to 240°, stirring occasionally, paying particular attention to the bottom of the pan.

Remove the pan from the heat and beat in the coffee extract and nuts. Cool a little, then beat until the mixture starts to leave a trail on itself.

Pour the fudge into the prepared pan. Leave to cool. Mark into squares as it begins to set. When completely cold and set, turn the fudge out and cut into the marked squares.

Chocolate and Hazelnut Fudge

A delightful creamy, nutty fudge, with a pleasing chocolate flavor.

6 cups confectioners' sugar

scant 1 cup evaporated milk

2 tablespoons unsalted butter

6 oz semi-sweet chocolate, grated

½ cup chopped hazelnuts

MAKES ABOUT 1¾ lb

Oil a 7-inch-square pan. Sift the confectioners' sugar into a large, heavy saucepan and add the milk and butter. Heat gently until the sugar has dissolved, stirring continuously. Bring to a boil and boil to 240°, stirring the mixture occasionally to prevent it from sticking and burning on the bottom of the pan.

Remove the pan from the heat, beat in the chocolate and nuts and continue to beat, if necessary, just until the mixture starts to leave a trail on itself.

Pour the fudge into the prepared pan. Leave to cool. Make into squares as it begins to set. When completely cold and set, turn the fudge out and cut into the marked squares.

Penuche

Penuche is a kind of fudge with a strong Mexican influence. It is harder than the usual fudge and darker in color. Because of the dark color, take particular care that it is not burning as it boils.

2⅔ cups light brown sugar

¾ cup milk

4 tablespoons unsalted butter

1 teaspoon vanilla extract

MAKES ABOUT 1½ lb

Oil a 7-inch-square pan. Put the sugar, milk and butter in a large heavy saucepan and heat gently until the sugar has dissolved, stirring continuously. The large grains of sugar are slow to dissolve, so take this stage carefully. Bring to a boil and boil to 240°, stirring occasionally.

Remove the pan from the heat, stir in the vanilla extract and beat well until thick and creamy.

Pour the mixture into the prepared pan. Leave to cool. Mark into squares as it begins to set. When completely cold and set, turn the fudge out and cut into the marked squares.

Peanut Penuche

Salted peanuts and peanut butter are used to obtain the delicious rich flavor of this fudge. The nuts are only roughly chopped to provide a good contrast in texture.

2⅔ cups light brown sugar	⅓ cup roughly chopped salted peanuts
¾ cup milk	
¼ cup smooth peanut butter	MAKES ABOUT 1½ lb

Lightly oil a 7-inch-square pan. Put the sugar, milk and peanut butter in a large, heavy saucepan and heat gently until the sugar has dissolved, stirring continuously. Bring to a boil and boil to 240°, stirring occasionally.

Remove the pan from the heat, stir in the chopped peanuts and beat well until thickened.

Pour the mixture into the prepared pan. Leave to cool. Mark into squares as it begins to set. When completely cold and set, turn the fudge out and cut into the marked squares.

Rum and Raisin Fudge

Rum-soaked raisins are always a popular flavoring. In this fudge recipe, the raisins are left to steep in the rum for 2 hours.

¼ cup raisins	1 cup heavy cream
2 tablespoons rum	2 tablespoons light corn syrup
2⅔ cups sugar	
1⅓ cups dark brown sugar	MAKES ABOUT 2 lb

Put the raisins and rum in a small bowl and leave to soak for about 2 hours. Just before making the fudge, oil a 7-inch-square pan.

Put the sugars, cream and corn syrup in a large, heavy saucepan and heat gently until the sugars have dissolved, stirring continuously. Bring to a boil and boil to 240°, stirring occasionally.

Remove the pan from the heat and stir in the rum and raisins. Cool a little, then beat until the mixture starts to leave a trail on itself.

Pour the fudge into the prepared pan. Leave to cool. Mark into squares as it begins to set. When completely cold and set, turn the fudge out and cut into the marked squares.

top SOUR CREAM AND BRANDIED APRICOT FUDGE (page 64); bottom CREAM AND CHERRY FUDGE (page 64)

Chocolate and Peppermint Fudge

This fudge has a lovely, soft texture. Its superb flavor is obtained by the addition of semi-sweet chocolate and peppermint extract. Avoid using artificial peppermint flavoring as this is a synthetic substitute and the taste of the fudge will be impaired.

2⅔ cups sugar	4 oz semi-sweet
⅔ cup milk	chocolate, grated
¼ cup honey	2 drops oil of peppermint
10 tablespoons unsalted	
butter	MAKES ABOUT 1½ lb

Lightly oil a 7-inch-square pan. Put the sugar, milk, honey and butter in a large, heavy saucepan and heat gently until the sugar has dissolved, stirring continuously. Bring to a boil and boil to 240°, stirring occasionally.

Remove the pan from the heat and leave on a cold surface, without stirring, for 5 minutes. Add the chocolate and peppermint extract and beat in until the chocolate is melted and the mixture starts to leave a trail on itself.

Pour the fudge into the prepared pan. Leave to cool. Mark into squares as it begins to set. When completely cold and set, turn the fudge out and cut into the marked squares.

Fruit and Nut Cream Fudge

The fruit and nuts in this tempting fudge recipe are raisins and toasted hazelnuts. After browning, the nuts are chopped, and provide a good texture contrast to the creamy fudge.

½ cup hazelnuts	1 cup heavy cream
3 tablespoons raisins	few drops of vanilla
1½ lb (4 cups) sugar	extract
2 tablespoons light corn	
syrup	MAKES ABOUT 2 lb

Spread the nuts on a baking sheet and lightly toast under the the broiler or in a preheated 400° oven for 5–10 minutes. Rub the nuts in a clean dish towel to remove the skins. Chop them and mix with the raisins in a small bowl. Lightly oil a 7-inch-square pan.

Put the sugar, corn syrup and cream in a large, heavy saucepan and heat gently until the sugar has dissolved, stirring continuously. Bring to a boil and boil to 240°, stirring occasionally.

Remove the pan from the heat, wait for the bubbles to subside and beat in the nuts and raisins and vanilla extract. Cool a little, then beat until the mixture starts to leave a trail on itself.

Pour the fudge into the prepared pan. Leave to cool. Mark into squares as it begins to set. When completely cold and set, turn the fudge out and cut into the marked squares.

Honey and Chocolate Fudge

The honey used in this recipe not only gives the fudge flavor, but stops it from crystallizing as well – making it deliciously soft and creamy textured.

2⅔ cups sugar
3 tablespoons honey
2 cups sweetened
   condensed milk
8 tablespoons (1 stick)
   unsalted butter

4 oz semi-sweet
   chocolate, grated
few drops of vanilla
   extract

MAKES ABOUT 1½ lb

Oil an 8-inch-square pan. Put the sugar, honey, condensed milk and butter in a large, heavy saucepan and heat gently until the butter has melted and the sugar has completely dissolved, stirring continuously. Bring to a boil and boil to 240°, stirring occasionally.

Remove the pan from the heat and beat in the chocolate and vanilla extract. Cool a little, then beat until the mixture starts to leave a trail on itself.

Pour the fudge into the prepared pan. Leave to cool. Mark into squares as it begins to set. When completely cold and set, turn the fudge out and cut into the marked squares.

Drambuie Dream

Drambuie, a whiskey and honey liqueur, turns this creamy fudge into an alcoholic dream – the perfect Christmas present.

1½ lb (4 cups) granulated
   sugar
1¼ cups heavy cream

2 tablespoons honey
1 tablespoon Drambuie

MAKES ABOUT 2 lb

Oil a 7-inch-square pan. Put the sugar, cream and honey in a large, heavy saucepan and heat gently until the sugar has dissolved, stirring continuously. Bring to a boil and boil to 240°, stirring occasionally, paying particular attention to the bottom of the pan in case the creamy mixture burns.

Remove the pan from the heat, wait for the bubbles to subside and stir in the Drambuie. Cool a little, then beat until the mixture starts to leave a trail on itself.

Pour the fudge into the prepared pan. Leave to cool. Mark into squares as it begins to set. When completely cold and set, turn the fudge out and cut into the marked squares.

Cashew Nut Fudge

Cashews have a light, subtle flavor often neglected by candymakers; toasting helps to emphasize it a little.

⅔ cup cashew nuts
2⅔ cups sugar
⅔ cup sweetened
    condensed milk
⅔ cup fresh milk

8 tablespoons (1 stick)
    unsalted butter
few drops of vanilla
    extract

MAKES ABOUT 1½ lb

Oil a 7-inch-square pan. Spread the cashews on a baking sheet. Lightly toast them under the broiler or in a preheated 400° oven for 5–10 minutes. Leave to cool, then split the nuts lengthwise along the natural break.

Put the sugar, milks and butter in a large, heavy saucepan and heat gently until the sugar has dissolved, stirring continuously. Bring to a boil and boil to 240°, stirring occasionally.

Remove the pan from the heat, add the toasted nuts and vanilla extract, then beat just until the mixture leaves a trail on itself.

Pour the fudge into the prepared pan. Leave to cool. Mark into squares as it begins to set. When completely cold and set, turn the fudge out and cut into the marked squares.

top ALMOND BRITTLE (page 69);
bottom MOLASSES TOFFEE (page 69)

Sour Cream Honey Fudge

You need an especially large saucepan for making this fudge as the mixture froths up as it cooks: do not use a pan less than 4 quart capacity.

1½ cups sour cream
¾ teaspoon baking soda
1½ lb (4 cups) sugar
3 tablespoons honey

3 tablespoons unsalted butter, cut into small pieces

MAKES ABOUT 2 lb

Lightly oil a 7-inch-square pan. Put the sour cream, baking soda, sugar and honey in a large, heavy saucepan. Stir well and leave to stand for about 20 minutes. Heat gently until the sugar has dissolved, stirring continuously. Bring to a boil and boil to 238°, stirring occasionally.

Remove the pan from the heat, stir in the pieces of butter and leave to stand for 5 minutes. Then beat until the mixture starts to leave a trail on itself.

Pour the fudge into the prepared pan. Leave to cool. Mark into squares as it begins to set. When completely cold and set, turn the fudge out and cut into the marked squares.

Sour Cream and Brandied Apricot Fudge

Soak ⅓ cup (2 oz) roughly chopped dried apricots in ¼ cup brandy overnight. Make as for Sour Cream Honey Fudge, beating in the apricots and brandy at the end. The large quantity of brandy makes this into rather a sticky, rich fudge.

Cream Fudge

This is a particularly rich and creamy fudge delicately flavored with vanilla.

1½ lb (4 cups) sugar
¾ cup heavy cream
1¼ cups milk

few drops of vanilla extract

MAKES ABOUT 2 lb

Oil a 7-inch-square pan. Put the sugar, cream and milk into a large, heavy saucepan and heat gently until the sugar has completely dissolved, stirring continuously. Bring to a boil and boil to 240°, stirring occasionally to prevent the milk and cream from burning on the bottom of the pan. As the mixture nears the correct temperature, lower the heat a little.

As soon as the temperature reaches 240°, remove the pan from the heat and stir in the vanilla extract. Wait until the bubbles subside, then beat until the mixture starts to leave a trail on itself.

Pour the fudge into the prepared pan. Leave to cool. Mark into squares as it begins to set. When completely cold and set, turn the fudge out and cut into the marked squares.

Cream and Cherry Fudge

Make as for Cream Fudge and add ⅓ cup (2 oz) chopped maraschino cherries when you beat it. (Dry the cherries well on paper towels before you chop them.) This mixture is rather slow to set. Leave overnight before turning the fudge out.

Pineapple Cream Fudge

This fudge has an unusual combination of flavor and texture. Pineapple extract and glacé pineapple are both used: you could, if you wish, make your own glacé fruit (see page 94).

1½ lb (4 cups) sugar
6 tablespoons unsalted butter
scant 1 cup evaporated milk
scant 1 cup fresh milk

few drops of pineapple extract
¼ cup chopped glacé pineapple

MAKES ABOUT 2 lb

Oil a 7-inch-square pan. Put the sugar, butter and milks in a large, heavy saucepan and heat gently until the sugar has dissolved, stirring continuously. Bring to a boil and boil to 240°, stirring occasionally.

Remove the pan from the heat and stir in the pineapple extract and chopped pineapple. Cool a little, then beat until the mixture starts to leave a trail on itself.

Pour the fudge into the prepared pan. Leave to cool. Mark into squares as it begins to cool. When completely cold and set, turn the fudge out and cut into the marked squares.

Date Squares

The higher-than-normal temperature used in this recipe gives a crisper textured fudge.

2⅔ cups sugar
⅔ cup milk
⅔ cup sweetened condensed milk
8 tablespoons (1 stick) unsalted butter

few drops of vanilla extract
¼ cup chopped dates

MAKES ABOUT 1½ lb

Oil a 7-inch-square pan. Put the sugar, milks and butter in a large, heavy saucepan and heat gently until the sugar has dissolved, stirring continuously. Bring to a boil and boil, still stirring, to 250°. Start boiling fairly quickly then lower the temperature and boil it very slowly toward the end.

Remove the pan from the heat, add the vanilla and dates and beat until the mixture starts to thicken and grain.

Pour the fudge into the prepared pan. Leave to cool. Mark into squares as it begins to set. When completely cold and set, turn the fudge out and cut into the marked squares.

Maple Cream Fudge

This tempting fudge, made with maple syrup, has a crisp texture. Make sure you use real maple syrup, not maple-flavored syrup.

2 cups maple syrup
1 tablespoon light corn
 syrup
⅔ cup heavy cream

1 teaspoon vanilla extract

MAKES ABOUT 1 lb

Oil a 6-inch-round pan. Put the syrups and cream in a large, heavy saucepan and bring very slowly to a boil, stirring continuously. Boil to 238°, without stirring.

Remove the pan from the heat, cool for 2 minutes then add the vanilla extract. Beat until the mixture starts to thicken.

Pour the fudge into the prepared pan. Leave to cool. Mark into diamonds as it begins to set. When completely cold and set, turn the fudge out and cut into the marked shapes.

Mocha Fudge

Chocolate and coffee are a traditional mixture in confectionery. Because the strength of coffee extracts vary, begin by adding one teaspoon then add more to taste.

1½ lb (4 cups) sugar
3 tablespoons light corn
 syrup
¾ cup milk
3 oz semi-sweet
 chocolate, broken into
 small pieces
pinch of salt

1–2 teaspoons coffee
 extract
6 tablespoons unsalted
 butter, cut into small
 pieces

MAKES ABOUT 2 lb

Oil a 7-inch-square pan. Put all the ingredients except the butter in a large, heavy saucepan and heat gently until the sugar has dissolved, stirring continuously. Bring to a boil and boil to 236°, stirring occasionally.

Remove the pan from the heat, add the pieces of butter and leave to stand for 5 minutes. Beat until the mixture starts to leave a trail on itself.

Pour the fudge into the prepared pan. Leave to cool. Mark into squares as it begins to set. When completely cold and set, turn out and cut into the marked squares.

BUTTERSCOTCH (page 72)

Toffees and Boiled Sweets

OFFEES are family-style candies – hardly elegant but nonetheless delicious. Real old-fashioned hard toffees or brittles are just as popular now as they were years ago. Made by boiling the sugar to very high temperatures, in the 290–310° region, they are brittle and the simple versions are clear and shiny. These toffees are so hard that you cannot cut them into neat pieces. They have to be broken with a hammer, so that the pieces all come out different shapes and sizes. When sucked they are inclined to go extremely chewy! For a gift, do not try and wrap individual pieces of old-fashioned toffee. Pack them in a square box in layers, between sheets of wax or baking parchment paper. They make a fun gift on Halloween or Thanksgiving.

Caramels are softer, often with cream or butter added for flavor. The temperature used to make them is not usually quite as high as that for toffee, so they are less brittle and can be cut up neatly. They are less hard on the teeth than English toffees, and are my personal favorites in this chapter. Then there is a whole range of other hard candies, all immensely popular and fun to make – barley sugar, mints and humbugs plus a wide variety of other possible flavors.

The temperature and humidity in the kitchen are important for all confectionery, but more so for toffees and other hard candies. In a damp atmosphere, toffees go sticky and cling to each other disastrously. So choose a dry day and try to keep the kitchen temperature at a comfortable 60–65°.

If possible, use an aluminum pan for making toffees and other hard candies. The temperatures are so high that it is all too easy to burn the syrup – aluminum will give the most even heat distribution and the best possible chance of avoiding scorching. As always, heat the sugar gently until dissolved, then raise the heat and keep it as even as possible until the required temperature is reached. Once the sugar has dissolved, do not stir unless the recipe specifically says to do so – stirring encourages the sugar to grain and the candies will be cloudy.

"Pulling," on the other hand, is a technique specially designed to make taffies opaque. If you tip the hot syrup onto a baking sheet instead of into a small pan, and allow it to cool a little, it can then be folded and pulled, twisted and generally handled until it becomes silky and quite different to look at. But do use rubber gloves for this process, as the mixture may still be very hot in the middle even if it seems to be cooling outside.

When you are pulling and twisting taffies, work quickly. One minute the mixture will be all soft and floppy, the next it will have hardened too much to cut. If possible have someone else standing by to help so that one of you can pull and twist while the other cuts. If the mixture does set before you have cut it, the taffy is not wasted. Put it on the baking sheet in a low oven for 3–4 minutes and you can work it again.

Store toffees and boiled sweets in a dry atmosphere at an even temperature. Cellophane wrappers and glass jars are often the most attractive way to present them.

Almond Brittle

A hard, golden toffee, packed with nuts. Ready-blanched almonds can be used but the flavor will not be as good.

1 cup almonds	few drops of almond
2⅔ cups sugar	extract
1¼ cups water	
pinch of cream of tartar	MAKES ABOUT 1¼ lb

Blanch the almonds in a bowl of boiling water for about 10 minutes. Cut them crosswise into halves. Dry thoroughly in a low oven, but without allowing them to brown.

Oil a 7-inch-square pan. Put the sugar and water in a large, heavy saucepan and heat gently until the sugar has dissolved, stirring continuously. Dissolve the cream of tartar in 2 teaspoons cold water and stir into the syrup. Bring to a boil and boil to 280°.

Remove the pan from the heat and stir in the halved almonds and a few drops of almond extract. Quickly pour the toffee into the prepared pan. Cool.

When completely hardened, turn the brittle out and break into pieces, using a small hammer or a rolling pin.

Molasses Toffee

This is a traditional hard, black toffee with a strong molasses flavor. It should be broken into pieces, using a small hammer. Old-fashioned kitchens were equipped with a toffee hammer for this purpose – about the size you might use for model making.

2⅔ cups dark brown sugar	⅔ cup sweetened condensed milk
⅓ cup molasses	1 tablespoon vinegar
⅓ cup dark corn syrup	
4 tablespoons unsalted butter	MAKES ABOUT 1½ lb

Oil an 11-×7-inch baking pan. Put all the ingredients in a large, heavy saucepan and heat gently until the sugar has dissolved, stirring continuously. Bring to a boil and boil, without stirring, to 280°. Pour into the prepared pan. Leave to cool.

When completely hardened, turn the toffee out onto a board and break roughly into pieces, using a small hammer.

Rum Honeycomb Toffee

A lovely dark color underneath, this toffee is clear as a jewel, with delightful, golden honeycombing on top.

2⅔ cups sugar	½ teaspoon baking soda
3 tablespoons dark corn syrup	1 teaspoon rum extract
1 tablespoon vinegar	MAKES ABOUT 12 OZ
⅔ cup water	

Oil a 7-inch-square pan. Put the sugar, corn syrup, vinegar and water in a large, heavy saucepan and heat gently until the sugar has dissolved, stirring continuously. Bring to a boil, without stirring, and boil to 310°.

When the mixture reaches 308°, remove from the heat, dissolve the baking soda in the rum extract and 2 teaspoons water and stir in. Make sure the temperature has risen to 310° and quickly pour the toffee into the prepared pan.

When completely hardened, turn the toffee out and break into pieces with a hammer. Store in layers between sheets of wax or parchment paper in an airtight container.

Honeycomb Toffee

A lovely crystal-clear amber toffee with a layer of yellow honeycombing on top.

2⅔ cups sugar	½ teaspoon baking soda
1¼ cups water	
¼ cup malt vinegar	MAKES ABOUT 1 lb

Oil a 7-inch-square pan. Put the sugar, water and vinegar in a large, heavy saucepan and heat gently until the sugar has dissolved, stirring continuously. Bring to a boil and boil, without stirring, to 285°.

Remove the pan from the heat. Dissolve the baking soda in 2 teaspoons water and stir into the toffee. Quickly pour the syrup into the prepared pan.

When the toffee is sufficiently set, mark it into small squares with a knife. When hardened, turn the toffee out and break along the marks.

Peppermint Toffee

This old-fashioned toffee has an unusual peppermint flavoring, and it is really very good.

2⅔ cups sugar
⅔ cup water
8 tablespoons (1 stick) unsalted butter

1 tablespoon vinegar
few drops of oil of peppermint

MAKES ABOUT 1 lb

Oil a 7 inch square pan. Put the sugar, water, butter and vinegar in a large, heavy saucepan and heat gently until the sugar has dissolved, stirring continuously. Bring to a boil and boil, without stirring, to 260°. Add a little peppermint extract and continue boiling to 280°.

Remove the pan from the heat and quickly pour the toffee into the prepared pan. Mark into squares with a knife as it begins to harden.

When completely hardened, turn the toffee out and break along the marks. Wrap in twists of wax or parchment paper and store in an airtight container.

Taffy

*The process of turning a clear syrup into this silky taffy, simply by folding and manipulating it, is absolutely fascinating. Children will love to watch you, but **do** keep them at a safe distance from the hot mixture.*

2⅔ cups sugar
⅔ cup water
8 tablespoons (1 stick) butter

pinch of cream of tartar

MAKES ABOUT 1¼ lb

Oil a baking sheet. Put the sugar, water, butter and cream of tartar into a large, heavy saucepan and heat gently until the sugar has dissolved, stirring continuously. Bring to a boil and boil, without stirring, to 280°. Quickly pour the mixture onto the prepared sheet and leave until you can handle it with rubber gloves.

Oil the rubber gloves, then fold the sides of the taffy to the middle and pull it out again. Keep folding and pulling until the taffy turns silky looking and opaque. Twist into long strips and cut into pieces with scissors. Leave to cool.

When completely cold and hard, wrap in twists of wax or parchment paper, cellophane or colored foil.

Peppermint Taffy

Add a few drops of oil of peppermint to the Taffy recipe, just before pouring it onto the baking sheet.

Anise Taffy

Add ¼ teaspoon anise extract to the Taffy recipe, just before pouring onto the baking sheet. This gives only a light flavor of anise. You could add more if you like a really strong taste.

Butterscotch

Butterscotch is a time-honored favorite, and this recipe has a particularly good buttery taste.

5 tablespoons unsalted butter, cut into small pieces

2⅔ cups light brown sugar

¼ cup dark corn syrup

1¼ cups water

MAKES ABOUT 1 lb

Oil a 7-inch-square pan. Put the butter, sugar, syrup and water into a large, heavy saucepan and heat gently until the sugar has dissolved, stirring continuously. Bring to a boil, without stirring, and boil to 290°, stirring just once or twice to make sure the butter is not sticking and burning on the bottom of the pan.

Remove the pan from the heat, stir lightly and pour into the prepared pan. Leave to cool. Mark into squares with a sharp knife as it begins to set. When completely cold and set, turn the butterscotch out of the pan and break along the marked lines.

Cream Caramels

The creamy flavor of these popular caramels is unmistakeable, and they are deliciously chewy too.

2⅔ cups sugar

1 cup light corn syrup

⅔ cup heavy cream

2 tablespoons unsalted butter

MAKES ABOUT 1¼ lb

Oil a 7-inch-square pan. Put the sugar and corn syrup in a large, heavy saucepan and heat gently until the sugar has dissolved, stirring continuously. Bring to a boil, without stirring, and boil to 265°.

Meanwhile, put the cream and butter in a small pan and heat gently to melt the butter. Add the cream and butter mixture to the syrup and boil again, stirring this time, until the temperature returns to 265°.

Remove the pan from the heat and pour the mixture into the prepared pan. Mark the caramel into squares as it begins to set.

When completely cold and set, turn the caramel out and break along the marked lines. Wrap each piece in wax or parchment paper. Leave to mature for two to three days before eating.

Vanilla Cream Caramels

When matured, these caramels are softer than the previous Cream Caramel recipe, chewy but not so hard on your teeth.

2 cups sugar	⅔ cup heavy cream
1½ cups light corn syrup	2 teaspoons vanilla
½ lb (2 sticks) unsalted	extract
butter	
⅔ cup milk	MAKES 1¼ lb

Lightly oil an 8-inch-square pan. Put the sugar, corn syrup, one third of the butter and all the milk in a large, heavy saucepan. Heat gently until the sugar has dissolved, stirring continuously. Still stirring, bring to a boil and add half the remaining butter. Boil, stirring, to 235°. Meanwhile, warm the cream slightly in a separate pan. Cut the remaining butter into small pieces.

Remove the pan from the heat and stir in the warmed cream, vanilla extract and remaining pieces of butter. Boil the mixture to 250°.

Pour the mixture into the prepared pan. Leave to cool. Mark into small squares as it begins to set.

When completely set, turn the caramel out and break into squares along the marked lines. Wrap each square in wax or parchment paper. Leave to mature for several days before eating.

Chocolate Coated Caramels

These milk chocolate-coated caramels are very soft and sticky when first made, and should be left for about two days to mature before eating.

2⅔ cups sugar	2 tablespoons unsalted
⅔ cup water	butter
⅔ cup light corn syrup	1 lb milk chocolate
⅔ cup heavy cream	
	MAKES ABOUT 2 lb

Oil a 7-inch-square pan. Put the sugar, water and corn syrup in a large, heavy saucepan and heat gently until the sugar has dissolved, stirring continuously. Bring to a boil and boil, without stirring, to 240°.

Meanwhile, put the cream and butter in a small pan and heat gently to melt the butter.

When the syrup reaches 240°, lower the heat slightly and add the warmed cream and butter mixture. Stir gently and continue boiling to 250°.

Pour the mixture into the prepared pan. Leave to cool. As soon as the caramel is firm enough to handle, turn it out of the pan and cut into very small squares with scissors. Once out of the pan the caramel will spread a little, and the pieces will end up bigger than you first cut them.

Break the chocolate into a bowl and melt it over a pan of hot water. Using a dipping ring, dip the caramels one at a time in the chocolate to give a generous coating. Place on parchment to harden. Leave to mature for two to three days before eating.

Chocolate Caramels

It makes a delicious change to flavor the caramels with chocolate instead of coating them in chocolate.

3 tablespoons unsalted butter	2 oz semi-sweet chocolate, grated
⅔ cup sweetened condensed milk	few drops of vanilla extract
1⅓ cups sugar	
⅔ cup light corn syrup	MAKES ABOUT 1 lb

Oil a 7-inch-square pan. Put the butter in a large, heavy pan and melt it slowly. Add the condensed milk, sugar and corn syrup and heat gently until the sugar has dissolved, stirring continuously. Bring to a boil and boil to 230°, stirring occasionally. Stir in the grated chocolate and boil to 255°, stirring.

Remove the pan from the heat and stir in a few drops of vanilla extract. Pour the mixture into the prepared pan. Leave to cool. Mark into squares with a knife as it begins to set.

When completely cold and set, turn the caramel out and break into squares along the marked lines. Wrap each square in wax or parchment paper. Leave for two to three days to mature before eating.

Old-Fashioned Humbugs

You can be quite generous with the coloring for this recipe as a strong color contrast makes the candies especially good.

2⅔ cups sugar	¼ teaspoon oil of peppermint
1 cup light corn syrup	brown food coloring
½ teaspoon cream of tartar	
1¼ cups water	MAKES ABOUT 1 lb

Lightly oil two baking sheets. Put the sugar, corn syrup, cream of tartar and water in a large, heavy saucepan and heat gently until the sugar has dissolved, stirring continuously. Bring to a boil, without stirring, and boil to 290°.

Remove the pan from the heat and add the oil of peppermint. Pour half the syrup onto each prepared baking sheet. Add about ½ teaspoon brown coloring to one portion. Leave until cool enough to handle.

Wearing oiled rubber gloves, fold and pull each portion until they become opaque and are starting to set. Roll each one into a long rod.

Lay the portions side by side and twist them together. Using scissors, cut off in ½-inch lengths. If the candy sets hard before you have finished shaping it, put the baking sheet in a 250° oven for 3–4 minutes until the mixture becomes workable again. When completely cold, wrap each piece in cellophane.

CHOCOLATE BRANDY TRUFFLES (page 80)

Fruit Drops

The confectioners' sugar in this recipe stops the fruit drops from sticking together. Pack them into a glass jar for maximum effect.

2⅔ cups sugar	yellow food coloring
1 cup light corn syrup	½ teaspoon orange extract
1 teaspoon cream of tartar	orange food coloring
¾ cup water	confectioners' sugar
½ teaspoon lemon extract	
	MAKES ABOUT 1 lb

Lightly oil two baking sheets. Put the sugar, corn syrup, cream of tartar and water in a large, heavy saucepan and heat gently until the sugar has dissolved, stirring continuously. Bring to a boil and boil, without stirring, to 310°.

Remove the pan from the heat and divide the syrup between the prepared baking sheets. Add about ½ teaspoon lemon extract and a few drops of yellow food coloring to one portion, and about ½ teaspoon orange extract and a few drops of orange coloring to the other. Leave until cool enough to handle.

Sift some confectioners' sugar into a bowl. Wearing oiled rubber gloves, fold and pull one portion to mix in the flavoring and coloring, then roll it into a stick. Cut off small portions with scissors and roll them between your hands to make small balls. Drop the balls in the confectioners' sugar to coat lightly, then remove them to cool.

Repeat with the other portion. If by the time you have worked the first batch the other has hardened too much to handle, put the baking sheet in a 250° oven for 3–4 minutes until the mixture becomes workable again.

Clear Mints

These cool, clear mints have a lovely light green color. Remember to handle the mixture quickly as soon as it begins to set, before it gets too hard to cut.

2⅔ cups sugar	½ teaspoon peppermint
¾ cup water	extract
1 cup light corn syrup	few drops of green food
	coloring
	MAKES ABOUT 1¼ lb

Lightly oil a shallow pan measuring about 11-×7-inches. Put the sugar, water and corn syrup in a heavy saucepan and heat gently until the sugar has dissolved, stirring continuously. Bring to a boil and boil, without stirring, to 310°.

Remove the pan from the heat and stir in the peppermint extract and a few drops of green food coloring.

Pour the syrup into the prepared pan. Leave to cool. As soon as the mint is firm enough to handle, turn it out with the help of a spatula and cut into squares with scissors.

Barley Sugar Twists

Many modern barley sugars are flavored only with lemon. This traditional recipe is made with real barley water.

2 tablespoons pearl barley	pinch of cream of tartar
5 cups water	
pared rind and juice of ½ lemon	MAKES ABOUT 1 lb
2⅔ cups sugar	

Lightly oil a baking sheet. Put the pearl barley in a saucepan with 1¼ cups of the cold water and bring to a boil. Drain and rinse under cold running water. Put the barley back in the pan with the remaining cold water and the lemon rind. Bring to a boil again, cover and simmer for about 2 hours.

Strain the barley liquid into a measuring cup and add the lemon juice and enough cold water to yield 2½ cups.

Put the sugar, cream of tartar and barley water in a large, heavy saucepan and heat gently until the sugar has dissolved, stirring continuously. Bring to a boil and boil to 290°.

Remove the pan from the heat and quickly pour the syrup onto the prepared baking sheet. Tilt the sheet to spread it evenly. Leave to cool a little.

As soon as the barley sugar is firm enough to handle, cut it into strips with scissors and twist each strip. Place on a board to finish cooling. The outside cools quicker than the middle, so work from both sides toward the middle, not straight from one side to the other. Wrap in twists of clear cellophane and store in a glass jar with an airtight stopper.

Buttered Brazils

Sweet, moist, fresh nuts are best for these favorite candies.

1⅓ cups light brown sugar	pinch of cream of tartar
4 tablespoons unsalted butter	6 tablespoons water
1 tablespoon light corn syrup	2 oz (½ cup) Brazil nuts
	MAKES ABOUT 12 oz

Lightly oil a baking sheet. Put the sugar, butter, corn syrup, cream of tartar and water in a small, heavy saucepan and heat gently until the sugar has dissolved, stirring continuously. Bring to a boil and boil to 280°, stirring occasionally.

Remove the pan from the heat. Using a dipping ring, quickly dip each nut into the mixture and place on the prepared baking sheet. Work as quickly as you can and reheat the syrup if necessary to keep it liquid. Leave until cold, then remove the buttered Brazils from the baking sheet and place in paper bonbon cases.

Petits Fours

HOWEVER good the dinner, a few petits fours offered with the coffee will make guests feel just that little bit pampered. But they are a fiddle to make, on top of everything else, so any hostess will delight in a gift box, all ready to serve. Pack a selection of fancy and plain ones together for maximum effect.

Marzipan Fruits

This is an excellent smooth paste, easy to mold and shape into fruits. The uncooked almond paste in the Almond-filled Fruits recipe is easier to make, but not as easy to mold, and it quickly cracks as it dries out.

2⅔ cups sugar	2 egg whites
⅔ cup water	1 cup confectioners' sugar
pinch of cream of tartar	a range of food colorings
2¼ cups ground almonds	
	MAKES ABOUT 2 lbs

Lightly oil a baking sheet. Put the sugar and water in a large, heavy saucepan and heat gently until the sugar has dissolved, stirring continuously. Bring to a boil, without stirring. Dissolve the cream of tartar in a little cold water, stir it into the syrup and continue boiling to 240°.

Remove the pan from the heat and beat until the sugar starts to grain. Stir in the ground almonds and egg whites. Cook gently over a low heat for a few minutes, stirring well.

Pour the mixture onto the prepared baking sheet. Sift the confectioners' sugar over and mix in, using a wooden spatula. When cool enough to handle, knead by hand until the paste is soft and pliable, adding a little extra confectioners' sugar if necessary.

When the marzipan is cold and smooth, break off small pieces and mold into tiny apples, bananas, oranges and so on. Use fine paint brushes and food colorings to tint them.

If you wish, you can knead coloring into a larger amount of marzipan to make the basis of several fruits. For example, color the marzipan yellow for bananas, green for apples, orange for oranges. After shaping, add shading to make each individual fruit more attractive. Leave to dry, then place in paper bonbon cases. Store in an airtight container.

Almond-filled Fruits

Quick and easy to make and unfailingly popular. Use dried or candied fruits, which will have a good cavity when the pit is removed.

1⅓ cups confectioners' sugar	1 egg, lightly beaten
⅔ cup granulated sugar	a selection of dried or candied fruits, eg. dates, figs, candied apricots, etc
1½ cups ground almonds	
½ teaspoon rum extract	sugar for coating

Sift the confectioners' sugar into a bowl and mix in the granulated sugar and almonds. Add the rum extract and enough of the egg to make a stiff paste. Knead by hand until smooth.

Press a small ball of almond paste into the center of each fruit. Roll the filled fruits in sugar. Leave to dry a little. Place in paper bonbon cases and store in an airtight container.

Chocolate Marzipan

Chocolate marzipan is made by kneading melted semi-sweet chocolate into the almond paste. Wrap them in squares of colored foil for maximum effect.

⅔ cups confectioners' sugar	few drops of almond extract
⅓ cup granulated sugar	lemon juice
¾ cup ground almonds	2 oz semi-sweet chocolate
½ medium egg	
	MAKES ABOUT 40

Sift the confectioners' sugar into a bowl and mix in the granulated sugar and almonds. Add the beaten egg, a few drops of almond extract and a little lemon juice and mix to a paste.

Break the chocolate into a bowl and melt it over a pan of hot water. Leave to cool, but not solidify, then add to the almond paste. Mix well, then knead by hand until smooth.

Roll out the marzipan to about ½ inch thick on a board dusted with sweetened cocoa powder. Cut into squares, using a sharp knife.

Nutty Figs

If stored for long, the sugar coating soaks in and the figs no longer look as pretty, though they still taste good. For a gift, prepare them ahead and roll in sugar just before packing. If you use frozen concentrated orange juice in the recipe, dilute it half and half with water.

1 lb whole dried figs	scant 1 cup blanched almonds
1¼ cups orange juice	
strip of lemon rind	
⅔ cup sugar	MAKES ABOUT 1½ lb

Put the figs in a saucepan with the orange juice, lemon rind and 3 tablespoons of the sugar. Heat gently until the sugar has dissolved. Bring to a boil and simmer for about 30–40 minutes until the figs are tender. Drain the figs and leave to cool.

Trim the stems off the figs and pierce the stem end of each one with a knife. Push an almond into the center and close the opening again by pinching it together with your fingers.

Roll the figs in the remaining sugar. Put on a wire rack to dry thoroughly. Place in wax paper cases and store in layers between wax or parchment paper in an airtight container.

Marzipan Neapolitans

These are pretty to look at and much simpler to make than the fruit shapes. The texture is smooth and you can flavor the marzipan, if you like – rum extract is good.

1⅓ cups granulated sugar	½ cup confectioner's sugar
5 tablespoons water	pink and green food colorings
pinch of cream of tartar	
1¼ cups ground almonds	
1 egg white	

MAKES ABOUT 26

Make the marzipan as for Marzipan Fruits (see page 78). Divide the marzipan into three portions. Tint one portion pale green, the second pink and leave the third portion plain.

Roll out each portion into a rectangle about ¼ inch thick measuring about 7×4½ inches on a board dusted with confectioners' sugar. Brush off any excess sugar and carefully place them one on top of the other – putting the plain portion between the colored ones. Using a sharp knife, trim the edges then cut the marzipan first into strips about 1 inch wide, then down into slices between ½ and ¾ inch thick. Place each one in a paper bonbon case and store in an airtight container.

Chocolate Brandy Truffles

Rich and irresistible, these truffles are made with crushed praline, chocolate, coffee, brandy and cream, then rolled in chocolate vermicelli.

2 oz (½ cup) unblanched almonds	8 tablespoons (1 stick) unsalted butter, cut into small pieces
⅓ cup sugar	3 tablespoons heavy cream
12 oz semi-sweet chocolate	chocolate vermicelli
½ cup strong black coffee	
1 tablespoon brandy	

MAKES ABOUT 30

Lightly oil a baking sheet. Put the almonds and sugar in a small saucepan and heat very gently until the sugar has completely dissolved, stirring continuously. Increase the heat and boil until the sugar turns a rich golden caramel color. Stir occasionally so the almonds color evenly.

Tip the caramel onto the prepared baking sheet. Leave to cool. When cold, chop the praline roughly, then grind it to an even powder in a blender, food processor or nut mill.

Break the chocolate into a bowl, add the coffee and brandy and melt over a pan of hot water. Remove from the heat, cool a little then gradually add the butter. When well blended, leave to cool until the mixture will leave a trail on itself if lifted. Gently stir in the praline powder and cream. Put in the refrigerator for about 8 hours or overnight.

Take a teaspoon of the truffle mixture at a time and shape into balls. Roll them in chocolate vermicelli and leave to set. Store in a cool place.

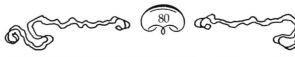

Madeira Truffles

Freshly made, these truffles are quite spectacular. After two or three days storage they are still acceptable, but more ordinary. Pound cake provides just the right crumb texture.

¾ cup ground almonds
2 cups pound cake
   crumbs
⅔ cup sugar
3 tablespoons apricot jam

about 3 tablespoons
   Madeira
sweetened cocoa powder

MAKES ABOUT 30

Put the ground almonds, cake crumbs and sugar in a bowl and mix together. Add enough apricot jam and Madeira to make a firmish mixture.

Take a small piece of the mixture at a time and roll into a ball. Toss the balls in cocoa powder to coat them thoroughly. Place in paper bonbon cases to harden. Store in an airtight container.

Langues de Chats à l'Orange

These tempting orange-flavored, piped petits fours are fairly soft in texture, rather like a sponge cake. They are best eaten on the day they are made.

4 tablespoons unsalted
   butter
3 tablespoons granulated
   sugar
½ egg
grated rind and juice of
   ½ orange

3 tablespoons all-purpose
   flour
⅔ cup confectioners'
   sugar, sifted
3 oz semi-sweet chocolate

MAKES ABOUT 15

Lightly oil a baking sheet. Cream 2 tablespoons of the butter and the granulated sugar together in a bowl until pale and fluffy. Beat in the egg and half the orange rind. Work in the flour until the mixture is of a piping consistency.

Spoon the mixture into a pastry bag fitted with a ½-inch plain tube. Pipe into fingers about 2½ inches long onto the prepared baking sheet, keeping them well spaced, as they will spread during cooking.

Bake in a preheated 425° oven for about 5 minutes until the edges just start to color. Lift onto a wire rack to cool.

Cream the rest of the butter and gradually beat in the confectioners' sugar, remaining orange rind and enough juice to make a cream of spreading consistency. Sandwich the cold langues du chats in pairs with the buttercream, shaping the edges neatly.

Break the chocolate into a bowl and melt it over a pan of hot water. Dip both ends of each langue du chat generously in the chocolate. Leave to dry on wax paper. Pack in an airtight container.

Hazelnut and Orange Meringues

These meringues are good served just as they are or they can be sandwiched with a little whipped cream. However, if you are giving them as a gift, remember that cream-filled meringues must be eaten within a few hours of assembling or they will go soft. If you are sure your gift will be eaten right away, make them up 2–3 hours before presenting them, otherwise leave them plain.

½ cup hazelnuts	few drops of orange extract
2 medium egg whites	semi-sweet chocolate
pinch of salt	
½ cup sugar	

MAKES 24–30

Brush two baking sheets lightly with oil and dust with sifted flour. Spread the hazelnuts on another baking sheet and lightly toast under the broiler or in a preheated 400° oven for about 10 minutes. Rub the nuts in a clean dish towel to remove the skins. Chop them finely and leave to cool. If you have used the oven to toast the nuts, reduce to the lowest possible temperature. If you used the broiler, preheat the oven to about 150° or its lowest setting.

Put the egg whites in a bowl with the pinch of salt and beat until stiff but not dry. Beat in a quarter of the sugar, 1 tablespoon at a time. Change to a large balloon whisk and continue whisking by hand until the meringue is smooth and glossy. Add a few drops of orange extract, the chopped nuts and remaining sugar and fold in evenly with a large metal spoon.

Using a teaspoon or a pastry bag fitted with a tube about ¼ inch in diameter, shape tiny mounds of the meringue on the prepared baking sheets. Bake in the oven at the lowest possible temperature for 60–70 minutes until crisp on the outside but still slightly soft in the center. Transfer the meringues to a wire rack to cool.

If desired the meringues may be coated in chocolate. Break the chocolate into a bowl and melt it over a pan of hot water. Add a few drops of orange extract. Dip the top of each meringue in the chocolate, without covering it completely, and return to the wire rack to set. Store in an airtight container.

top ECLAIRS AU CAFÉ (page 86); bottom HAZELNUT AND ORANGE MERINGUES (above)

Almond and Coffee Meringues

Delicious, delicate little meringues, with a buttery covering topped with shiny icing.

1 egg white
3 tablespoons ground almonds
3 tablespoons sugar
1½ oz tablespoons all-purpose flour
2 tablespoons finely chopped almonds, to decorate

Buttercream
6 tablespoons unsalted butter
2 cups confectioners' sugar
2 teaspoons instant coffee
1–2 tablespoons hot water

Glacé icing
1⅓ cup confectioners' sugar
2 tablespoons instant coffee
2 tablespoons hot water

MAKES ABOUT 18

Lightly oil a baking sheet and dust with sifted flour. Beat the egg white in a bowl until stiff and firm. Sift the ground almonds, sugar and flour together and fold into the egg white, using a metal spoon.

Spoon the mixture into a pastry bag fitted with a ¼-inch plain round tube. Pipe the meringue mixture in 1½-inch lengths onto the prepared baking sheet. Bake in a preheated 375° oven for 7–8 minutes. Lift onto a wire rack and leave to cool.

To make the buttercream, cream the butter until soft and gradually sift and beat in the confectioners' sugar. Dissolve the instant coffee in 1 tablespoon of the hot water. Beat into the buttercream, add a little more hot water if necessary to achieve a working consistency.

Cover each meringue with a smooth mound of buttercream and leave to harden.

To make the icing, sift the confectioners' sugar into a bowl. Dissolve the coffee in the hot water and gradually add to the confectioners' sugar until the icing will coat the back of a spoon thickly.

Hold each meringue in your fingers and dip into the icing to coat the top and right down the sides, covering the buttercream. Put the iced meringues on a wire rack, decorate each one with a small pinch of chopped almonds and leave to set. Store in an airtight container.

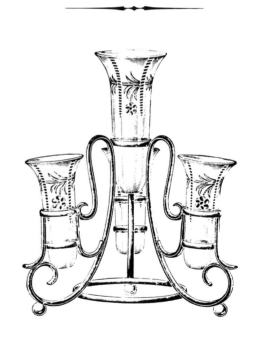

Almond and Pistachio Fingers

An intriguing blend of light, nutty flavors. Finely chopped pistachios are made into a paste with fragrant orange flower water, then sandwiched between a layer of almond paste and baked. Before cutting into fingers, the baked nut mixture is browned under the broiler.

1½ cups ground almonds
2 cups confectioners' sugar
1 tablespoon rose water
½ egg white

4 oz (1 cup) shelled pistachios
1 tablespoon orange flower water

MAKES 24

Mix the ground almonds, confectioners' sugar and rose water with a fork until they bind together. Add the egg white and continue to mix until a paste forms. Knead by hand until smooth.

Blanch the pistachios in a bowl of hot water for about 10 minutes. Remove the skins, then finely chop the nuts in a blender or food processor. Mix the pistachios and orange flower water to a paste.

Divide the almond paste in half. Spread half of it evenly over the bottom of a 7-inch-square shallow pan, using your fingers to spread it to the corners. Spread the pistachio paste over the top. Cover with the remaining half of the almond paste, smoothing the surface with a spatula.

Bake in a preheated 375° oven for 10 minutes. Place the pan under a hot broiler for about 2 minutes to brown. Turn the almond and pistachio cake out into the broiler pan and brown the other side. Leave to cool. When cold, cut into 1-inch wide fingers. Store in an airtight container.

Palmiers

The secret of the shaping of these tempting pastries lies in the clever folding and cutting of the puff pastry.

4 oz puff pastry
granulated sugar, for dredging

confectioners' sugar, for dusting

MAKES 18

Roll out the pastry very thinly to a neat rectangle 6×8 inches. Trim the edges straight with a sharp knife. Dredge the surface of the pastry with granulated sugar. Fold in the long edges to meet in the center. Dredge with granulated sugar again and fold in half again lengthwise. Press lightly with the rolling pin to seal the layers together.

Cut the pastry into slices about ¼ inch thick and place on a baking sheet. Open the centers out slightly to make a heart shape.

Bake in a preheated 425° oven for 5–6 minutes until the pastry is well puffed and the sugar a light caramel color. Turn the palmiers over and cook for a further 2–3 minutes until crisp and golden. Lift the pastries onto a wire rack and dust with sifted confectioners' sugar before they are completely cold. Store in an airtight container.

Eclairs au Café

The pastry shapes can be made well in advance and kept in an airtight container, or even frozen, but once filled with cream they must be eaten within a few hours.

2 tablespoons unsalted butter	2 teaspoons instant coffee
5 tablespoons water	2 tablespoons hot water
¼ cup all-purpose flour	½ cup heavy cream
1 medium egg, beaten	
1⅓ cups confectioners' sugar	MAKES 15

Sprinkle a baking sheet with water. Put the butter and water in a saucepan and bring to a boil. Sift the flour onto a sheet of wax paper. When the butter mixture boils, remove the pan from the heat and tip in the flour all at once. Beat with a wooden spoon until the paste is smooth and comes away from the sides of the pan to form a ball in the center. Allow to cool for 1–2 minutes.

Beat the egg into the paste, a little at a time, using a wooden spoon. Beat until smooth and shiny.

Spoon the mixture into a pastry bag fitted with a ⅜-inch plain round tube. Pipe tiny éclairs about 1–1½ inches long on the prepared baking sheet, cutting the paste off cleanly with a wet knife for each one.

Bake in a preheated 400° oven for 7 minutes until well risen. Increase the oven temperature to 425° and bake for a further 5 minutes until crisp and golden.

Slit each éclair down the side with a sharp knife to allow the steam to escape, then return them to the oven for 1 minute to dry. Transfer to a wire rack.

Sift the confectioners' sugar into a bowl. Dissolve the coffee in the hot water. Gradually stir the liquid coffee into the confectioners' sugar until the icing is smooth and glossy and coats the back of a spoon. Spoon a little over the top of each cooled éclair.

Shortly before serving, whip the cream and pipe or spoon into the éclairs.

Coconut Thins

Lovely thin, crisp, tasty cookies that keep surprisingly well in an airtight container.

2 tablespoons unsalted butter	3 tablespoons shredded coconut
3 tablespoons sugar	1 teaspoon lemon juice
1½ tablespoons light corn syrup	
3 tablespoons all-purpose flour	MAKES 20

Oil two to three baking sheets. Cream the butter and sugar in a bowl until pale and fluffy. Beat in the corn syrup. Stir in the flour, shredded coconut and lemon juice.

Take about ½ teaspoon of the mixture at a time, roll into a small ball and place on the prepared baking sheets, spacing them well apart.

Bake in a preheated 325° oven for about 7 minutes until the edges are golden brown and the centers lightly colored. Leave for a few moments on the baking sheets to harden. Lift them onto a wire rack, using a spatula. When cold, store in an airtight container.

top ALMOND AND PISTACHIO FINGERS (page 85);
bottom LANGUES DE CHATS À L'ORANGE (page 81)

Petits Fours à la Génoise

A génoise mixture is always good for a cake you want to keep. These store well, becoming moister as the days go by.

⅔ cup all-purpose flour
pinch of salt
3 tablespoons unsalted
  butter
3 eggs
½ cup granulated sugar
apricot glaze
4 cups confectioners'
  sugar
1–2 tablespoons warm
  water

To decorate
crystallized violets
silver balls
nuts

MAKES 40

Lightly oil an 11-×7-inch baking pan and line the bottom neatly with parchment paper. Oil the paper, then dust the paper and sides of the pan with flour.

Sift the flour twice with the salt and set aside. Warm the butter gently to melt, then leave to cool but do not let it solidify again. Break the eggs into a large bowl and gradually beat in the granulated sugar. Place the bowl over a pan of hot water and beat for about 10 minutes until the mixture is very thick, light and slightly warm.

Remove the bowl from the heat and continue beating until the mixture cools and leaves a trail on itself. Resift the flour a little at a time onto the egg mixture and fold in lightly with a metal spoon. Add the melted butter, a little at a time, folding in carefully.

Pour the mixture into the prepared pan. Bake in a preheated 350° oven for 25–30 minutes until the cake slightly shrinks away from the sides of the pan. The center should spring back if lightly pressed with a finger. Leave to cool for a few minutes in the pan, then turn out onto a wire rack until completely cold.

When cold, use a serrated edge knife to cut the cake into small squares, about 1 inch each. Return them to the wire rack. Brush each one with a little warm apricot glaze.

Sift the confectioners' sugar into a bowl and gradually stir in the warm water until the icing is smooth and glossy. Quickly spoon the icing over the little cakes and top with a variety of decorations, such as crystallized violets, silver balls, or nuts.

Miniature Florentines

Deliciously crunchy, with a smooth chocolate backing, these are classic cookies. Tiny ones make good petits fours.

1 heaping tablespoon
  roughly chopped glacé
  cherries
1 tablespoon finely
  chopped candied peel
½ cup chopped mixed
  nuts
¼ cup slivered almonds

3 tablespoons unsalted
  butter
⅓ cup sugar
1 tablespoon heavy cream
4 oz semi-sweet chocolate

MAKES 25

Line two baking sheets with parchment. Put the cherries, candied peel and chopped and slivered nuts in a bowl. Melt the butter in a small saucepan, stir in the sugar and heat gently until dissolved. Bring to a boil and pour onto the fruit and nut mixture. Add the cream and stir until thoroughly mixed in.

Using no more than 1 teaspoon at a time, place little mounds of the mixture on the prepared baking sheets, spacing them well apart.

Bake in a preheated 350° oven for 5 minutes. Remove from the oven and shape up each one into a neat round, using a 2-inch cookie cutter. Return the cookies to the oven for 3 minutes, then shape them again. Cook for a final 1 minute. If necessary, just tidy the edges again. Leave the cookies on the baking sheets until they are just beginning to set, then lift onto a wire rack to cool.

Break the chocolate into a small bowl and melt it over a pan of hot water, stirring until smooth. Remove the pan from the heat, but leave the bowl over the hot water.

Using a small spreader, spread chocolate over the smooth side of each cookie, then place them chocolate side up on the wire rack to set. Before the chocolate dries, mark in the traditional wavy lines, using a decorating comb or fork.

Miniature Brandy Snaps

Brandy snaps can be eaten plain or filled with whipped cream, but cream should not be added until shortly before serving, as it will soften them.

2 tablespoons unsalted butter	drop of vanilla extract
3 tablespoons light brown sugar	3 tablespoons all-purpose flour
1½ tablespoons light corn syrup	tiny pinch of salt
¼ teaspoon lemon juice	¼ teaspoon ground ginger
	MAKES 18

Thoroughly oil a baking sheet. Put the butter, sugar and corn syrup in a small saucepan and heat gently until the butter has melted and the sugar dissolved. Leave to cool slightly. Add the lemon juice and vanilla extract, then sift in the flour, salt and ground ginger. Stir until thoroughly mixed.

Spoon the mixture ½ teaspoon (no more) at a time, onto the prepared baking sheet; spacing each spoonful about 3 inches apart. Leave the remaining mixture in the saucepan.

Bake in a preheated 325° oven for 5–6 minutes. Leave to cool on the baking sheet for 1–2 minutes. Working quickly, lift each one in turn off the baking sheet with a spatula and wrap it, flat side inwards, around the handle of a small wooden spoon. Leave for a few moments to harden then slide the brandy snap off and place on a wire rack. If the cookies on the baking sheet harden too much, put them back in the oven for a few seconds.

Clean and oil the baking sheet, then repeat the process until all the mixture is used up. Do not bake two sheets at once; it makes the job too hectic when shaping. When cold, store in an airtight container.

Brandied Shortbread

*Those who prefer something plain after dinner
will love this. It is moist but still crumbly.*

1⅓ cups all-purpose flour	1 tablespoon brandy
½ cup fine semolina	few drops of brandy
12 tablespoons (1½ sticks)	extract
unsalted butter	2 tablespoons blanched
½ cup + 1½ tablespoons	almonds
sugar	
	MAKES 24

Sift the flour and semolina together. Cream the
butter, ½ cup of the sugar, the brandy and extract
together in a bowl. Mix in the flours to give a fairly
sticky paste.

Spoon the paste into a 7-inch-square shallow pan
and mark into fingers. Split the blanched almonds
along the natural break and scatter them over the
top. Sprinkle with the remaining sugar.

Bake in a preheated 375° oven for 15–20 minutes
or until just set and a very pale golden color. Leave
to cool in the pan. Turn the shortbread out and
break into slices along the marks. Store in an airtight
container.

Spiced Sugared Almonds

*These sugared almonds are crisp, not hard like
the purchased variety. If you prefer, the
cinnamon may be omitted.*

½ cup blanched almonds	syrup stock (see page 42)
½ lb (1 cup) basic fondant	orange food coloring
(see page 42)	
¼ teaspoon ground	MAKES 50
cinnamon	

Spread the almonds on a baking sheet and lightly
toast under the broiler or in a preheated 350° oven
for about 10 minutes. Leave to cool.

Melt the fondant in a bowl over hot water (see
page 44), avoiding overheating. Add a little syrup
stock if necessary to achieve a coating consistency.
Add the cinnamon and tint the fondant a pale
orange color.

Using a dipping ring, dip the almonds, one at a
time, into the fondant. Place on parchment to dry.

GLACÉ FRUIT (page 94)

Candied Fruits

SUGAR, in high concentrations, is a marvelous preservative. Candying is a method of steeping fruit in sugar to such an extent that the natural deterioration of the fruit is slowed almost to a halt. As a bonus, it results in a highly luxurious confection. There are few people who could fail to be delighted with a gift of home-made candied fruits.

The process works by gradually increasing the concentration of sugar within the fruit. This has to be done slowly – an initial dipping would simply result in the sugar coating the outside of the fruit. By successive applications of heat, by gradually increasing the density of the syrup and by long periods of soaking, the sugar is persuaded to penetrate every fiber of the fruit.

Candied Fruit

This technique takes at least 16 days, demanding just a small amount of attention each day. No wonder candied fruits are so expensive to buy! The results, however, are well worth the trouble.

fresh fruit, such as oranges, apricots, pineapple, kiwi, pears, apples	sugar 2 tablespoons orange flower water

Day 1
Choose firm, ripe fruits, free from blemishes. Small fruits can be left whole but if they have tough skins

– such as plums or apricots – prick them all over with a fork; or halve them and remove the pits if you prefer. Remove the pits from cherries with a cherry pitter. Remove the peel from citrus fruits and divide oranges into segments, removing all pith and membrane. Peel pears, apples and peaches and halve them or cut into thick slices. Go over pineapple carefully to remove all the skin, core and "eyes;" you can either cut the pineapple flesh into chunks or rings.

Weigh the fruit after preparation but before cooking. Always candy different types of fruit separately, so that they retain their individual flavors.

Put the prepared fruit in a saucepan, just cover with boiling water and simmer gently until just tender. Take care not to overcook the fruit, as soft fruits will have less taste and will lose their shape. On the other hand, if you undercook the fruit the finished product will be tough.

For every 1 lb prepared fruit, use 1 cup sugar and 1¼ cups of the water the fruit was cooked in.

Lift out the fruit carefully from the cooking liquid with a slotted spoon and place it in a large bowl. Do not heap the fruit up too much or the pieces at the bottom will get squashed – try to choose a wide bowl so that the fruit does not lie too deep.

Dissolve the sugar very slowly in the water, stirring continuously with a metal spoon. Bring to a boil and pour the syrup over the fruit. The fruit must be completely covered with syrup; if it isn't, make up more syrup of the same strength, but remember to increase the amount of sugar used on subsequent days in the same proportion. Leave to soak for a full 24 hours.

Day 2

Drain off the syrup into a saucepan and add another ⅓ cup sugar. Dissolve it slowly over gentle heat, stirring continuously. Bring to a boil and pour the syrup back over the fruit. Soak for another 24 hours.

Days 3–7

Repeat that step every day for the next five days, so that the syrup gradually gets stronger and stronger.

Days 8–9

At the beginning of the second week, drain off the syrup and add ½ cup sugar (instead of the ⅓ cup you have been adding up to now). Dissolve it and then add the fruit to the syrup in the pan; simmer gently for 3–4 minutes. Carefully return the fruit and syrup to the bowl. Leave to soak for a full 48 hours.

Day 10

Repeat the same procedure with ½ cup sugar. Then add 2 tablespoons orange flower water and leave to soak for four full days. This is the last soaking and you can leave it longer if you wish, up to about two weeks; the fruit becomes sweeter and sweeter, the longer it is left.

Finally, drain off the syrup and spread the pieces of fruit out on a wire rack. Place the rack on a tray and cover the fruit without touching it: use an inverted roasting pan, a loose tent of foil, a plastic box – just to protect it from dust, flies etc. Leave the fruit in a warm place such as a warm corner of the kitchen until thoroughly dry – about two to three days. Turn each piece two or three times while drying.

When completely dry, carefully pack the candied fruits in boxes with wax or parchment paper between each layer.

Glacé Fruit

The glacé process adds a crisp, glossy coating of sugar to the original preserved fruit.

---

candied fruit (see page 92)

2⅔ cups sugar

⅔ cup water

The candied fruit must be thoroughly dry. Put the sugar and water in a saucepan and dissolve the sugar slowly over a gentle heat, stirring. Bring to a boil and boil for about 1 minute.

Pour a little of the syrup into a small bowl and keep the rest warm over hot water. Put a little boiling water in another bowl.

Using a dipping fork or skewer, dip the candied fruit, one piece at a time, into the boiling water for about 20 seconds, then into the syrup. Place on a wire rack to dry. Replace the boiling water as it cools, and the syrup as it becomes cloudy. Dry the fruit again for two to three days, turning occasionally.

Index